Study Guide

THE
MARRIAGE
CODE

BILL & PAM
FARREL

HARVEST HOUSE PUBLISHERS
EUGENE, OREGON

Published in association with the literary agency of Alive Communications, Inc., 7680 Goddard Street, Ste #200, Colorado Springs, CO 80920. www.alivecommunications.com.

Cover design by Left Coast Design, Portland, Oregon

Cover photograph © Mark Evans/iStockphoto

THE MARRIAGE CODE STUDY GUIDE
Copyright © 2009 by Bill and Pam Farrel
Published by Harvest House Publishers
Eugene, Oregon 97402
www.harvesthousepublishers.com

ISBN 978-0-7369-2184-8

Printed in the United States of America

09 10 11 12 13 14 15 16 / VP-SK / 10 9 8 7 6 5 4 3 2 1

Contents

How to Get the Most Out of This Study Guide

You have in your hands a devotional study guide for *The Marriage Code.* This is your personal guide for learning how to discover the code that makes your marriage work well. Three guiding principles drive the process in this book.

The first is: *You have a code.* Your code is a combination of usernames and passwords that grant you access to the best parts of your relationship. When these codes are in place, your relationship appears to be relatively easy. The way you interact, love, argue, and make decisions is satisfying for you as a couple. When the code is missing, all the systems of your relationship are awkward. You fail in your attempts to connect emotionally, your love for each other is elusive, and you seem to disagree on just about everything.

The second guiding principle is: *Get above the line.* The exclusive nature of marriage creates a fascinating dynamic. The key needs of *success* for the husband and *security* for the wife can be triggered quickly. A wife can instantly feel secure or she can instantly feel insecure. A husband, likewise, can feel suddenly successful or suddenly like a failure.

It's as if you operate in your marriage around a line. When your key need gets met, you move above the line and *everything* seems to work well. You are comfortable in the relationship, you forgive readily, you find it easy to give your spouse the benefit of the doubt, and romance is satisfying. When your key need gets threatened, you immediately move below the line and *everything* seems to be a problem. The relationship feels awkward, most discussions turn into arguments, you entertain thoughts about your spouse's motives that are petty and selfish, and you fight the urge to blame your spouse for your dissatisfaction.

The strangest part of this dynamic is that you can move above the line or below the line very quickly. One word, one action, one look can ruin the atmosphere of your relationship and send you plummeting below the line. Trust is temporarily lost and feelings are bruised. In the same way, one word or action can elevate you above the line, reestablish trust, and normalize the atmosphere in your home.

The third guiding principle is: *You have a helper.* The Holy Spirit brings with Him a deep love for your spouse and insight into every one of the codes that will unleash the potential of your marriage. When you make a personal decision to begin a relationship with God, God sends His Spirit to live in your soul so that He is there to whisper new thoughts, new ways, and new insights that will enhance your life and all your relationships. Since God takes up residence in your heart and mind, you no longer have to muddle through life and the relationship puzzle alone. The God who personally designed each of you is there to give you direction.

The exercises in this study guide are designed to help you discover your code and get above the line of trust by accessing the wisdom and power of the Holy Spirit in your relationship with your spouse. The exercises are organized to help you develop a pattern of growth that will lock in your code and help you establish a love for one another that is both secure and successful. You can work on the exercises at your own pace to maximize their influence in your relationship. They are organized as weekly pursuits, but you can do them faster or slower, depending on your preference. The exercises consist of:

Quick Review. Each chapter has a short recap of the content from *The Marriage Code* as a reminder to get you in the mood for the study.

Strategic Prayer. Each chapter contains a written prayer that relates to the topic for the week. By reciting this prayer each day during your study of each chapter, you will reinforce the process of growth.

Code Search: A Look in the Word. Each week, key Bible verses are introduced that correspond to the topic. These verses will help you explore the truth about the Holy Spirit and how He works in our lives.

God's Help to Get Above the Line. Following the verses is a discussion of a practical skill for letting the Holy Spirit guide and strengthen you to love your spouse and thrive in your marriage. These skills are based on our study of Scripture and personal experience in our marriage and ministry. Our prayer is that these discussions make the power of the Holy Spirit more accessible to you as you seek to develop a secure and successful marriage.

Practice the Presence. We have also included practical exercises so you can practice accessing the resources of the Holy Spirit. We recognize that for many of you, these skills are new and may be awkward to implement. The good news is that these are skills that through practice can be moved from awkward to effective.

As you study the verses in this guide and work on these skills, we encourage you to keep a journal of your insights and accomplishments. We have discovered that writing out prayers to Jesus and journaling our feelings are a safety valve for our relationship. Each of you should have your own journal so that your thoughts and feelings can remain private, although you are free to share any you wish. Often, if you write out your feelings, plans, and ideas before you talk about them, God sheds new light on the situation. You may discover new ways of interacting or new areas of growth you can work on. Or perhaps you will gain a new insight into your spouse that builds compassion or cooperation. When I (Pam) journal, I first pray and ask God to lead me as I write. Then I reread the Scripture for the day and ask:

- Is there a command to obey?
- Is there a principle to observe?
- Is there a sin to confess?
- Is there a praise to express?

In other words, what does God want me to *do* as a result of reading this section of Scripture? Then after I write down my thoughts, I reread them and ask, "What have I learned?"

When I (Bill) journal, I ask God to slow me down enough to think about what is really going on in my life. I read the Scripture for the day and pray: *God, help me think clearly today. Give me the insight I need to function well in my marriage today. You know exactly what I need to learn in order to function at my best, so please speak to my heart and help me be open to what will make me my best today.* I then write out the thoughts that come to mind in response to the verses I have read and the questions for the day.

A Little Bit of Fun. In each chapter, we have included stories and jokes just to remind all of us not to take ourselves too seriously. We have made a habit of telling people, "We want you to take your wedding vows seriously, but we don't want you to take yourselves too seriously." There is no perfect marriage, but the right balance of skills, dedication, and laughter can make your love a growing experience.

Decoder Moments. Each chapter in *The Marriage Code* contains stopping points to apply the skills you are learning. The study guide contains reminders and preparation exercises to help you be more successful in your interactions.

Getting Ready for Dinner. Each chapter in *The Marriage Code* also contains a "Dinner and Dialogue" exercise to help you apply the skills of the chapter. The study guide contains reminders and preparation exercises to help you get ready for your weekly date.

We recommend that as a couple you set a time each week to complete this activity together. You might want to have a quick bite of breakfast together, and then enjoy the guide as a devotional aid. Or you may want to meet during dinner or perhaps at bedtime, if that works better in your schedule. The key is to do this weekly. Don't let the busyness or the responsibilities of your life keep you from the progress you can make in your relationship.

Love Letter. At the end of each week, we recommend you write a letter to your spouse telling him or her what you have learned about yourself and your relationship. We will encourage creativity in this step through various prompts. We suggest you read your letters to each other during your "date night." There is power in hearing, then receiving, words of love and affirmation. When your spouse reads the letter again later, he or she can hear your voice in each word you've written. Don't be concerned that you have to be some grand poet or write a long letter. The sincerity of your heart is more important than the technique you use.

We will give you writing prompts each week. Feel free to use these to kick-start your imagination. But also feel free to completely ignore them and just write whatever you want. This is your golden opportunity each week to share your heart, and however you decide to share is good. Keep in mind that this is the best place to give encouragement because the positive words can be read over and over again. And since the written word is so powerful, it may be the *worst* place to share negative feelings because they also can be read over and over, each time wounding your mate again.

We know that constructive criticism must be shared at times, but it is best shared in an environment where love is thriving. We believe, therefore, that it is best to write out our negative feelings and pray over them privately before we *verbally* share them with each other. Sometimes we decide not to share them at all after we have written out our feelings and prayed over them. When we do share them with each other, the time we took to prepare slows us down so we can cautiously direct our body language and facial expressions with the goal of sharing the truth *in love*.

This date night is also a wonderful opportunity to do the "Unlocking the Code: Dinner and Dialogue for a Heart-to-Heart Connection" at the end of each chapter in *The Marriage Code*. Your once a week date night can become a light at the end of the tunnel. Each week, the goal of your date night is to connect romantically. The "Unlocking the Code" questions and the sharing of love letters is a wonderful way to layer love into your life. By creating this positive foundation weekly, tough issues become easier to tackle because there is an atmosphere of security and love in your relationship.

Overall, the best way to a break the code in your marriage is to grow as a lover and partner in life. This study guide is designed to strengthen and equip you as an individual as it deepens and strengthens your love. Your faith in God will grow, and from that reservoir, you will gain the ability to be a conduit of God's love toward your spouse.

This is a fun adventure of love—enjoy the adventure!

Chapter 1

In Search of the Marriage Code

It is a whisper, not audible but clear:

"Pam, tell Bill thank you."

"Bill, help Pam out; she is stressed."

"Pam, wait to bring that up. Bill has his hands full right now."

"Bill, wrap your arms around her, she's afraid. She's trying to be brave, but she needs strength."

"Pam, Bill needs you. Stop what you're doing right now and go to him."

The whisper isn't heard with one's ears but in one's heart and soul. The whisper is the code breaker. The whisper is God's Spirit. The whisper is the secret to moving and keeping your relationship "above the line" and a love that is "above the line" is sweet.

And sometimes that whisper shouts to keep us from making a big mistake.

Don went to a lawn-equipment store to look at used riding mowers. After examining the array, Don wanted to think about it. Not wanting to lose a sale, the sales manager quickly mentioned their 60-day, no-interest payment program.

"Sounds great," Don said. "But I have to talk this over with my wife or there'll be a 60-days, no-interest at home."

The whisper moves us away from marital danger and disaster and moves us closer to one another. So how do you hear the whisper?

QUICK REVIEW

The main point of chapter 1 is that the marriage code is based on the most common needs that men and women have. Men are primarily looking for a relationship that is successful while women are primarily looking for a relationship that is secure.

- *Security* is the belief that it is safe to be who I am.
- *Success* is the belief that my life is workable.

When success and security are present in the marriage, the relationship moves above the line of trust and makes almost everything in the relationship smooth out.

STRATEGIC PRAYER

As you study this chapter, pray this prayer each day this week to focus your heart on the possibilities in your marriage.

> Dear Lord, we can be confident in our love because You are near us (Philippians 4:5) and the joy of the Lord is our strength (Nehemiah 8:10). God, since You are love and You live in us, we have the ability to love each other. In fact, we love because You first loved us (1 John 4:7, 19). Thank You for the gift of the Holy Spirit. We already have everything we need for life and godliness, and it is secured by Jesus Himself (2 Peter 1:3-4). We realize that apart from You we can do nothing, but with You all things are possible (Matthew 19:26; John 15:5). Please fill us with Your Spirit and give us Your power for our lives and our love. Amen.

CODE SEARCH:
A Look in the Word

Each week, we will have you look into God's Word to learn a new skill to better tune into the leading of the Holy Spirit. When you are connected to the Spirit's leading, it is easier to keep your marriage above the line. As you get to know God's Spirit and how God works and leads, you are better able to follow, and then God can give you the vital access codes to your spouse's heart because God can trust that you will use this vital information to bless, encourage, and affirm your mate. In encouraging your mate, you are able to decode your mate and build a love to look forward to.

You can do each lesson in one sitting or break it up into a few minutes every day. Either way, the Spirit will be able to whisper to your heart because you will be listening. Let's begin.

Read Ephesians 5:21-33

> Submit to one another out of reverence for Christ.
>
> Wives, submit to your husbands as to the Lord. For the husband is the head of the wife as Christ is the head of the church, his body, of which he is the Savior. Now as the church submits to Christ, so also wives should submit to their husbands in everything.
>
> Husbands, love your wives, just as Christ loved the church and gave himself up for her to make her holy, cleansing her by the washing with water through the word, and to present her to himself as a radiant church, without stain or wrinkle or any other blemish, but holy and blameless. In this same way, husbands ought to love their wives as their own bodies. He who loves his wife loves himself. After all, no one ever hated his own body, but he feeds and cares for it, just as Christ does the church—for we are members of his body. "For this reason a man will leave his father and mother and be united to his wife, and the two will become one flesh." This is a profound mystery—but I am talking about Christ and the church. However, each one of you also must love his wife as he loves himself, and the wife must respect her husband.

Note: Submission is a military term that represents a voluntary decision by one officer to rank himself or herself under another officer in order to accomplish a mission. Submitting to God and the Spirit is a choice. Submitting in marriage is a choice. When we choose to meet each other's core need and move our marriage above the line, we are choosing to submit, most importantly, to God's plan.

How does it help a man feel more successful when his wife chooses to help him accomplish the things in life that are important to him?

What can you do this week to help your husband feel more successful?

Husbands are challenged to love their wives. What sacrifices did Christ make to show His love for the church? What sacrifices can a husband make to help his wife feel more secure?

What can you do this week to help your wife feel more secure?

In the phrase "washing with the water of the word," the term for spoken word is used and represents statements a husband makes to build up his wife. How do these kinds of statements help a woman feel more secure?

List phrases that you can tell your wife this week that might make her feel more secure:

In verse 33, wives are challenged to respect their husbands. How is respect related to submission? How does a wife's respect help a man feel more successful?

What are things you can do this week or things you can say this week to show respect to your husband?

In verse 32, Paul points out that the relationship between a husband and wife is a reflection of the love relationship between Jesus and the church. How does the church (you, your spouse, and others who believe in Jesus) help Jesus succeed on earth with His mission?

How does Jesus help believers feel more secure during their journey on earth? How does having a relationship with Christ help you feel more secure?

Read 1 John 1:9

> If we confess our sins, he is faithful and just and will forgive us our sins and purify us from all unrighteousness.

What are we challenged to do in this verse?

What happens in our lives when we do this?

What do you think might happen in your love life if you listened to God's Spirit and confessed (or agreed with God) so your view of life and love matched God's view?

Read Ephesians 5:18

> Do not get drunk on wine, which leads to debauchery. Instead, be filled with the Spirit.

What is God's will for you according to Ephesians 5:18?

Why do you think being filled with Holy Spirit is compared to being under the influence of alcohol in this verse?

What do you think would happen in your life and in your love if you were completely under God's influence?

Read I John 5:14-15

> This is the confidence we have in approaching God: that if we ask anything according to his will, he hears us. And if we know that he hears us—whatever we ask—we know that we have what we asked of him.

Describe in your own words what these verses mean.

What is God's response when you ask Him to do something He already wants to do?

Since it is God's will that your marriage be full of love, unity, meaning, and fulfillment, then what will He do if you ask Him for help to accomplish that goal?

Take a few moments right now to ask God to help you in your marriage.

GOD'S HELP TO GET ABOVE THE LINE:
Walking in the Power of the Holy Spirit

Pam and I met when we were in college at a student leadership conference with Campus Crusade for Christ. That organization was influential in helping us learn how to trust in the power of the Holy Spirit. Bill Bright, the founder of Campus Crusade for Christ, taught a concept called "Spiritual Breathing" that was especially helpful. We learned that spiritual impurities must be exhaled and spiritual nutrients must be inhaled in order to have a healthy spiritual life.

The spiritual impurities are what the Bible calls sin, which is any act of self-will that diverts us from accomplishing God's will. When we become aware of these acts of self-will, the Bible tells us to "exhale" by "confessing our sins" (1 John 1:9). As we journey through our lives, the Holy Spirit will point these sins out to us. He is so interested in us experiencing His strength in our lives that He stirs us up when there is a sin holding us back. The Holy Spirit will use various means, but He will make us aware of the specific thoughts, attitudes, and actions that prevent us from being filled with His power.

We see some disturbing results of following our impulses in life. When we give in to these desires, the Holy Spirit stirs us up. The purpose of disturbing us, however, is not to make us feel guilty. It is to get us to confess. Confession has three simple steps:

1. *Admit* what you did to God. Don't explain it or justify it. Simply admit that your thought, action, or attitude was contrary to God's will.

2. *Agree* that what you did was wrong. Romans 3:23 is very clear when it comes to admitting our shortcomings, "All have sinned and fall short of the glory of God." When you admit what you did was wrong, you guide your heart to be cooperative with God.

3. *Apologize* to your Savior. The first step to real change is a contrite heart. If you admit to something but are not sorry

for it, you are not really confessing. You might be sorry only that you got caught. Being sorry you got caught is not repentance; you need to also be sorry you made the wrong decision in the first place. If you are not sorry or do not apologize, then you are hardening your heart toward this action or attitude which will all but guarantee that you will do it again and again.

Once you have exhaled, it is time to inhale. Dr. Bright explains that we inhale by appropriating the power of the Holy Spirit into our lives. We are commanded to be filled with the Holy Spirit in Ephesians 5:18. Being filled is different from being indwelt. The Holy Spirit lives in every believer, but not every believer is yielded to His guidance.

This is a very dynamic process. Every decision in our lives affects who is in charge of our lives. It is just like driving a car. Every time you as a couple get in a car, you have to decide who will drive. In the same way, you have been given the privilege of deciding who is "driving your life" each and every day. You can be in charge and rely on *your* wisdom, skills, insight, and experience. Or you can put the Holy Spirit in charge and make *God's* wisdom, skills, power, and guidance active in your experience.

Like breathing, we must do this daily. The process of inhaling is based on a simple, biblical concept. God wants us to say yes to His will, and it is His will for you be filled with Holy Spirit.

First John 5:14-15 profoundly says that God will say yes to His will. Ephesians 5:18 makes it clear that it is God's will for us to be filled with the Spirit. Notice the parallel here between the influence of alcohol and the influence of the Holy Spirit. We believe the parallels are linked to three ideas. Alcohol will cause you to do things you wouldn't normally do, say things you wouldn't normally say, and give you boldness that is not normally characteristic of you. In the same way, the Holy Spirit will help you say things and do things that are highly strategic, and you will have boldness in your love to unselfishly serve and encourage your spouse.

It follows, then, that if we ask God to fill us with His Spirit, He will say yes. This is inhaling. The only thing that can prevent the Holy Spirit from being in charge is our sin. When we become aware of any sin in our life, we can confess it and set up our heart to be empowered by the Spirit once again. This is exhaling.

When we consistently exhale and inhale, we will become comfortable with the Spirit in the driver's seat, and we will grow increasingly dissatisfied when we take the wheel. Love is so much better, stronger, sweeter when God is in the driver's seat. After all, He designed love in the first place. Invite God, the author of love, into the control seat of your marriage and see what real love can look like.

PRACTICE THE PRESENCE

Each day this week:

- Ask God, "Is there anything I need to confess to You today?"
- Confess anything that comes to mind.
- After you have confessed, ask God to fill (empower) you with His Spirit.
- At the end of your day, write down the ways you noticed that God worked in your life.
- If you see any ways God's Spirit enhanced your marriage or helped you better love your mate or helped you be a better spouse, thank God the moment you recognize that blessing.

DECODING DELIGHT:
Enjoy a little bit of fun together

Each week you will be encouraged to go on a date. You don't have to go out; these dates can easily happen at home. Just clear space in your schedule once a week for a little quality time with the one you love. These dates will be easier to enjoy if you both commit to doing the study guide and the preparation pieces for the date. Is it a little work? Sure. But aren't you, your spouse, and your love life worth it? We think so!

GETTING READY FOR DINNER
Preparation for Your Dinner and Dialogue Assignment

On page 27 in *The Marriage Code*, we encouraged you to meet your spouse in a relaxed environment and discuss the questions below. To prepare for this time together, set a time and place with your spouse, and then write out your thoughts in the space provided:

Husbands, your wife will be asking you the following two questions:

- What things do I do that help you feel more successful?
- What days so far in our relationship have you felt most successful?

  Write down a list of traits in your wife that make you feel more successful so you can thank her for these qualities when you meet:

Wives, your husband will be asking you the following two questions:

- What things do I do that help you feel more secure?
- What days so far in our relationship have you felt most secure?

  Wives, write down a list of traits in your husband that make you feel more secure so you can thank him for these qualities when you meet:

LOVE LETTER

Each week there will be a love letter prompt. After you write the letter, select a romantic time and place to read the letter aloud, then hand a copy to your spouse for him or her to keep. Words are more powerful when shared out loud and more lasting when one can read them over and over. Write the first letter to your spouse by finishing these thoughts:

- My life is better with you in it because…
- I believe we are going to have a great year this year as we…
- I have been praying for you, and this year I am asking God to…

Chapter 2

The Mystery of Love

"The fruit of the Spirit is…love…"

Sometimes our differences divide us.

One Thursday evening, a young couple came into the luggage department of the store where I work. They could not agree on one large suitcase or two smaller ones. Their disagreement grew into a full-fledged shouting match and culminated with the woman storming out of the store. The man, still steaming, approached my register and said, "We want the large suitcase."

"Why not wait until next week when the piece you want will be on sale?" I suggested, hoping to defuse the tense situation.

"We can't wait," he replied. "We're leaving for our honeymoon on Sunday."[1]

But it was also your differences that first attracted you to each other. Think back, what is one thing about your spouse that first attracted you to him or her? (Make a list of things that first attracted you that are very different from who you are. This list will come in handy later.)

QUICK REVIEW

The main point of chapter 2 is that love is a mystery because you have married someone who is thoroughly different from you. Your differences increase the potential of your life so that you can accomplish more and experience more than you could have as an individual. As you learn to appreciate and trust these differences, the likelihood that your marriage will move above the line increases.

STRATEGIC PRAYER

As you study this chapter, pray this prayer each day this week to focus your heart on the potential of your relationship.

> Dear God, help us to laugh together and encourage each other as we face the responsibilities of our week. Help us to find ways to sacrifice for one another this week so that our marriage can be a reflection of Your love. We are convinced there is nothing that can prevent us from the success that honors You the most because You are for us (Romans 8:31-32). We, as a couple, can experience this success because You have promised to meet all our needs and to carry on to completion the work You began in us (Philippians 1:6; 4:19). Give us the grace to let Your love flow through us to each other. Amen.

CODE SEARCH:
A Look in the Word

Read Genesis 1:27

> So God created man in his own image,
>   in the image of God he created him;
>   male and female he created them.

There are two key thoughts in the creation of mankind: (1) we are made in the image of God, and (2) we were created male and female.

From what you know about the male gender, what can you conclude about the image of God?

From what you know about the female gender, what can you conclude about the image of God?

Read I Corinthians 2:9-11

> However, as it is written:
>
> > "No eye has seen,
> >   no ear has heard,
> > no mind has conceived
> >   what God has prepared for those who love him"—
> > but God has revealed it to us by his Spirit.
>
> The Spirit searches all things, even the deep things of God. For who among men knows the thoughts of a man except the man's spirit within him? In the same way no one knows the thoughts of God except the Spirit of God. We have not received the spirit of the world but the Spirit who is from God, that we may understand what God has freely given us.

Let's break it down to see what the Spirit can do:

What does the Spirit reveal (vv. 9-10a)?

What does the Spirit search (vv. 10b-11)?

So we could understand what (v. 12)?

What results can I anticipate in my life with this kind of wisdom?

Read Ephesians 1:17

> I keep asking that the God of our Lord Jesus Christ, the glorious Father, may give you the Spirit of wisdom and revelation, so that you may know him better.

What type of Spirit has been given to us according to this verse?

What can you expect to happen in your life with this type of Spirit in you?

Read Isaiah 11:2-3

> The Spirit of the LORD will rest on him—
>> the Spirit of wisdom and of understanding,
>> the Spirit of counsel and of power,
>> the Spirit of knowledge and of the fear of the LORD—
> and he will delight in the fear of the LORD.

What type of Spirit has been given to us according to these verses?

What can you expect to happen in your life with this type of Spirit in you?

GOD'S HELP TO GET ABOVE THE LINE:
Cooperating with the Holy Spirit

The fact that you are working through this study guide probably means you hope to build a strong marriage that works for both you and your spouse. You have plans, and you are a person who cares about doing your best. This can be a challenge, however, when you merge your life with someone who is very different from you.

This is where learning to cooperate with the Holy Spirit's leading is strategic. Following the Spirit's lead involves planning and adjusting because there is nothing passive about following! We encounter a very active partnership between people and God in Proverbs 16.

> ¹To man belong the plans of the heart,
>> but from the LORD comes the reply of the tongue.

⁷When a man's ways are pleasing to the LORD,
   he makes even his enemies live at peace with him.

⁹In his heart a man plans his course,
   but the LORD determines his steps.

³³The lot is cast into the lap,
   but its every decision is from the LORD.

We are challenged to plan our ways with our hearts fully invested in what we want to do. God wants us to search our hearts for the activities, decisions, and pursuits that matter to us. At the same time, "The LORD directs our steps." God did not motivate you with talent and desires only to leave you to your limited perspective. God actively watches over your life and prompts you to make adjustments to your plans as necessary. He coaches us up.

Having coached all my kids in basketball, I (Bill) appreciate the connection between athletes exercising their talents while the coach directs their steps. The youth league we were a part of had a rule that all kids would play half the game. Well, one year we had a young man on our team who was coordinated and enthusiastic, but he was very distracted. Let's call him Tom. He had a hard time concentrating and did not have the ability to follow the plan we were trying to implement. In a word, Tom was different from everyone else on the team. He had his own way of doing things, and there was no changing him. As the coach, I could see that the whole team was frustrated with him, but I had to play him half the game.

Seeing the need for a major adjustment, I asked God to give me a creative idea. I was working in the yard at home, and I saw a fly buzzing around my head. I thought, *That fly reminds me of this kid. He is always busy, makes strange noises, and is kind of irritating. I wonder if I can create a new defense that will keep him busy while the rest of the team plays basketball?*

I explained to the team at the next practice that we were going to play a special defense for two quarters of the game that was sure to drive the other team crazy. I told the team that the name of this defense was "The Fly Defense," and Tom is the fly. I then looked at Tom and said, "You are the key to this defense. I want you to picture yourself as a fly on the court. Your job is to run around and try to land on the basketball any time the other team has the ball. Do you think you can do that?"

With a gleam in his eye he said, "You bet, Coach. I'll do it."

Well, it worked. He ran around the court like a kid at recess who had sat for too long in class. He even made a buzzing sound at times. The other team didn't know what to do with this kid because no one plans an offense to overcome a fly on the court. Tom took his new-found importance to heart and worked extremely hard.

I don't want to suggest that any of you are overactive or distracted, but you are trying to build a life with someone who is different from you. As a result, there are adjustments that need to be made that will not occur to you. The Holy Spirit knows just what adjustments need to be made, and He will reveal them to you when the time is right. And because the Spirit is God, the creator, His ideas will be more creative than what you might come up with on your own. Your job is to make plans, get in motion, and be willing to adjust.

Recently God's Spirit led us to a creative way to avoid conflict. Once during a busy time, when days were packed with responsibilities of work, church, kids, and community, I (Pam) was feeling a little lonely and neglected, so I started to whine to God.

Lord, I wish Bill would send me a card.

Lord, I wish Bill would walk in and slide his arms around my waist.

Lord, I wish Bill would whisk in and kidnap me so we could just grab a little escape and laugh a little.

Lord, I miss Bill sexually.

Why isn't Bill making me a priority?

Then the whisper came, "Why don't you do these things for Bill that you want for yourself. Give and trust that I (God) will out give you."

So each time I wished Bill would do something for me, I would instead do it for him. Bill had no idea that God and I had this challenge going on, which made it so much sweeter when Bill began to be himself again, doing all the nice, thoughtful things that are consistent with who he is normally. Had I demanded that Bill do these things, it could have placed a wedge between us, or the gestures might have felt contrived or insincere. Instead, God moved my heart to give sincerely, and the fruit was God moved Bill's heart to move sincerely too. A win/win—that's what God is best at.

Psalm 37:4-5 echoes this same thought:

> Delight yourself in the LORD
>   and he will give you the desires of your heart.
> Commit your way to the LORD;
>   trust in him and he will do this.

In addition to getting into motion, we need to plan with an attitude of prayer. In other words, we need to invite God to our planning meetings. Committing our way and trusting in the Lord means we have asked God for wisdom in our planning, and we have asked the following questions:

- Are my plans based on what I know about God?
- Is this something that God would reasonably be in favor of?
- Would I be glad to meet God face-to-face while I'm doing what I am about to do?
- Can I enthusiastically ask God to make this happen?

When you can sincerely say yes to these questions, God gives you the green light and will get actively involved to accomplish His will in your life. When these questions bother you, it's time to slow down and take your decision back to the drawing board.

"Delight yourself in the LORD and He will give you the desires of your heart." This is where following the Spirit's lead becomes highly relational. Many tasks need to be accomplished in life, but life is more than tasks. Life is also about love, intimacy, encouragement, hope, and inspiration. When we take our plans to God with the attitude that He is more important than our plans, new possibilities open up for us. God begins to open our heart to the dreams He has for us. Since

His perspective is much larger than ours, He sees opportunities that would never occur to us. We will never discover them on our own, and when we are first exposed to them, they will seem uncomfortable or even impossible. But our success when we choose to engage in these revealed ventures will be amazing because we are now experiencing what we once thought impossible.

I (Bill) had to go through one of these major adjustments with our middle son, Zachery. He is a talented young man. He is physically strong and agile, and he has a gift for relating to people. In high school, I assumed he would play football and pursue physically demanding challenges. I was stunned when one day he announced, "I want to be a cheerleader." I had never considered this before. When I was growing up, young men became cheerleaders because they couldn't do anything else, and they were more comfortable around girls than other young men. My first thought was, *This cannot be happening!*

A statement I had made, however, kept running across my mind. It was one of those nagging thoughts that just won't go away. It was like a musical tune that gets stuck in your head and just won't leave you alone. The statement was, "I will fully support my kids in their pursuits no matter what they choose (as long as it's not illegal or immoral)." As much as I wanted it to be, cheerleader was neither immoral nor illegal. I came to the conclusion that I needed to learn more about cheerleading.

I discovered, of course, that cheerleading has changed a lot since I was young. It is highly competitive and similar to gymnastics. It is actually amazing to me now to watch these young men execute lifts and throws with their female partners to the fast-paced music. I'm glad I adjusted because cheerleading has provided a big life for my son in college. He attended the University of Louisville where he has gone to the Final Four, the Orange Bowl, and the Gator Bowl. The team was even approached by Circus de Soleil to see if any of them wanted to perform during the pregame of the Super Bowl. About the time I got used to my son being a cheerleader, he joined the circus! I never thought I would love the cheer world, but it has been an amazing journey for my son.

The Spirit can help you adjust to your mate's differences too.

Bill: Pam is spontaneous. Sometimes she springs ideas on me and that can frustrate me, but the Spirit reminds me that my life would be boring without her in it.

Pam: Bill is cautious by nature. Sometimes I am prone to resent the slower pace until the Spirit reminds me that God gave me Bill to help me be more prudent and thoughtful.

Bill: Pam is a woman of faith. She always believes God will provide, which is admirable until I try to get the checkbook to balance. Then God's Spirit reminds me that a good portion of our income is a direct result of Pam's faith. Our writing and speaking might never have gotten off the ground without her optimism.

Pam: Bill is a man of integrity. He is a man who takes a stand on the truth. Rules matter to him. This is all great until one of the rules seems frivolous or superficial to me, then the Spirit reminds me that Bill's strong inner compass has helped me develop a stronger grid for making wiser decisions.

The key is to make plans, but don't get stubborn. Keep your heart open to adjusting when the Spirit makes it clear that a change of course is best.

PRACTICE THE PRESENCE

Practice cooperating with the Spirit this week. Choose the minor decisions of your life to work with. Since this is practice, you want to start with choices that are simple and comfortable as you develop your skill. With each small decision, remember to ask these questions:

- Are my plans based on what I know about God?

- Is this something that God would reasonably be in favor of?

- Would I be glad to meet God face-to-face while I am doing what I am about to do?

- Can I enthusiastically ask God to make this happen?

As you discover "Yes" answers to these questions, commit whole-heartedly to your plans. If you sense a "No," adjust your plans and consider another course of action. When a new path occurs to you, ask the same questions. Remember this is practice, so God may take you through a few drills to increase your skill. As you grow comfortable with the skill, you can begin to apply it to the more important decisions in your life.

DECODING DELIGHT:
Enjoy a little bit of fun together

Decoder Moments

On page 34 in *The Marriage Code,* we encouraged you to "chat about the gender differences that you appreciate most in your mate." Make a list of the ways your spouse is different from you. Choose two or three and write down why you appreciate this difference. (You can look back to the list of things that first attracted you to your mate.)

On page 46, we encouraged you to identify "what advice has someone older and wiser given you on marriage that you have seen rings true?" Write below the advice you can remember:

GETTING READY FOR DINNER
Preparation for Your Dinner and Dialogue Assignment

Choose a trait based on your spouse's gender and compliment him or her every day for a week. Choose the ways you plan to deliver this compliment:

- ☐ Verbally
- ☐ E-mail
- ☐ Voicemail
- ☐ Written notes
- ☐ Text messages
- ☐ Greeting cards
- ☐ Facebook
- ☐ Twitter
- ☐ Other _____

I will assign the following trait in my spouse's life to the slow-growth category (see pages 46-47 in *The Marriage Code* for our discussion of slow-growth traits):

LOVE LETTER

Write a letter to your spouse that begins with this statement:

- "I love the fact that you are different from me in the following ways…"

Chapter 3

Affection

"The fruit of the Spirit is...kindness..."

We all long for affection, and we are usually willing to do almost anything to keep a loving environment in our marriage.

One panicked husband needed a creative idea. He was caught in gridlocked traffic, his cell phone was dead, and it was his anniversary. Knowing the whole evening would be wrecked if he was late and didn't call, he wrote a message on some paper he had in the car and taped it to his rear window, asking the passing motorists to help a guy out.

When he finally arrived home, his wife gave him a passionate, lingering kiss, and he knew his night would be good as she said, "You must really love me. Fifty people must have called me in the past hour to tell me so."[2]

So how can the Spirit help us decode our mate to keep the love environment of our intimate life red hot?

QUICK REVIEW

The main point of chapter 3 is that you have been created to respond to affection. It makes you feel stronger, more confident, and attractive. You can cultivate affection in your marriage by kindly touching each other, by focusing on your spouse's unique ability, and by showering your relationship with kind words.

STRATEGIC PRAYER

As you study this chapter, pray this prayer each day this week to raise your affection level.

> Dear Lord, we know that each of us was once unkind because we were foolish, disobedient, deceived, and enslaved to various lusts and pleasures (Titus 3:3). Then the kindness of Jesus appeared, and we were saved (Titus 3:4-5). Please use this kindness in our lives to enhance our love. Because of Your kindness, we have an eternal relationship with You, and we have been led to repentance (Romans 2:4). We have been adopted as Your children (Ephesians 1:5), and we have been given insight into the mystery of Your will (Ephesians 1:8-9). As a result, we can now look out for the interests of others and treat them as more important than ourselves (Philippians 2:3-5). Please guide our steps this week so that others benefit from what You have done in our lives. Amen.

CODE SEARCH:
A Look in the Word

Read Hebrews 3:13

> But encourage one another daily, as long as it is called Today, so that none of you may be hardened by sin's deceitfulness.

What daily activity should we engage in according to Hebrews 3:13?

What happens when we engage in this activity?

Thinking back, write down the encouraging statements you have made to your spouse in the last 24 hours:

On a scale of 1 to 10, 10 being most encouraging, mark how encouraging you think you have been to your mate in the past week (circle number): 1 2 3 4 5 6 7 8 9 10

One of the main descriptions of the Holy Spirit is "Counselor." According to Jesus in John 14:16,26 and 15:26, what does the Holy Spirit do for you as your Counselor?

John 14:16

> "And I will ask the Father, and he will give you another Counselor to be with you forever—"

John 14:26

> "But the Counselor, the Holy Spirit, whom the Father will send in my name, will teach you all things and will remind you of everything I have said to you."

John 15:26

> "When the Counselor comes, whom I will send to you from the Father, the Spirit of truth who goes out from the Father, he will testify about me."

In what area of your marriage do you need some good counsel?

Read Zechariah 4:6

> So he said to me, "This is the word of the LORD to Zerubbabel: 'Not by might nor by power, but by my Spirit,' says the LORD Almighty."

What areas of your life need the Spirit's attention rather than your own power and might?

What did the Holy Spirit pour into us according to Romans 5:5? "And hope does not disappoint us, because God has poured out his love into our hearts by the Holy Spirit, whom he has given us."

How does this impact your ability to encourage your lover?

What is one area that you especially need God's power (not just your own) to show affirmation, affection, and encouragement to your mate?

Take a moment right now and ask God to empower you to be affectionate or affirming to your mate about this issue.

GOD'S HELP TO GET ABOVE THE LINE:
The Encouragement of the Holy Spirit

Encouragement is one of the most powerful gifts God gave us in our relationships. Encouragement provides a daily focus that leads to a positive attitude, selfless interaction, and appreciative partners. We all live in a world that is trying to harden us. Difficulties and disappointments seek to steal the vitality out of our lives. If we are not careful, our hearts grow hard, our passions grow dull, and our appetite for truth grows cold.

The antidote for cold hearts is a lifestyle of encouragement. Unfortunately, most of us have a soft view of encouragement. We tend to think of it as nice words, "You are doing great. I am proud of you. I am behind you—way behind you, but I am behind you." To be sure, words are a vital part of encouragement, but they are not the complete story. One of the Greek words translated "encouragement" in the Bible is a compound word made up of two other words. The first word is *para*, which means "alongside of." The second word is *klesis*, which means "a calling." *Paraklesis*, therefore, means, "called alongside another individual."

The implication, especially in marriage, is that you are committed to bring out the best in the other person. You will use kind words if that will help your spouse feel better about life. You will offer your assistance if that will help your spouse succeed. You will back off and let your spouse approach a pursuit alone if that will help your spouse grow. You will confront your spouse if that will help your spouse reach his or her potential. It won't matter to you what it takes. You will be motivated by the thought that you can help your partner be the person God designed him or her to be.

Encouragement is so powerful because you go into partnership with the Holy Spirit when you encourage your spouse. The word translated "Counselor" or "Helper" in the verses above from the gospel of John is also a compound Greek word, and it is a cousin to the word *paraklesis*. The word here is *parakletos*, which means "one who is called alongside." Jesus could just as easily have called the Holy Spirit "The Encourager," because that is what He does in our lives. He is called alongside your spouse and is committed to bring out the best in your lover.

When you commit to the same process, your small efforts join together with the big efforts of the Holy Spirit, and the hearts of those you love soften. Because of who the Holy Spirit is (The Encourager), He is committed to help you love your spouse. He will make suggestions to you about what you can say or do to make your spouse feel more confident and gain energy for the pursuits of life.

It starts with the words that are all around you and from a variety of sources.

Pam and I decided that our favorite relationship song is "Unforgettable," written by Irving Gordon and made famous by Nat King Cole.

Pam has been a speaker for women's events for a number of years, so we spend many weekends apart. One day this song came on the radio, and the thought jumped out at me, *Bill, any time you hear this song and are not with Pam, you should call her and hold your phone to the speaker. That way she'll know she is loved even though you are apart.* I am sure I did not come up with that idea on my own, and it has been a winner. Just the other day, Pam was in the Eastern time zone while I was in the Pacific time zone. It was ten o'clock at night when I left a meeting and drove home. Our song came on the radio, so I called Pam. It was one in the morning her time, and as soon as I heard her sleepy voice, I moved my phone to the speaker. When I held the phone to my ear again, I heard a very sleepy, "Thanks, honey. I love you."

The Spirit will also suggest acts of kindness for you to do for your spouse. All of us live responsible, challenging lives that sometimes get out of our control. At these times, a helping hand or a kind gesture have a way of lightening the load and resurrecting hope. As you go about your daily responsibilities, certain suggestions will occur to you that will encourage your spouse and enhance the value of your relationship.

When Bill was working as a senior pastor, he had a habit of saying "Wow!" whenever he came across something in a sermon that he loved. It caught on with the whole congregation. People would respond to statements in the service with "Wow!" Every children's program included a "Wow" reaction written into the script for the cast to shout at a specific moment in the production. I was looking for a way to encourage Bill, so I prayed for days. It then occurred to me that a "Wow" tie tack would be a great gift, and it was right on the mark. It instantly became his favorite tie tack.

Every once in a while, the Spirit is going to whisper something unique in your ear. We like to call these "brilliant moments" because they are instances of unusual creativity. You will probably be amazed that you even came up with the idea as it becomes a memory that lingers throughout the years.

I (Pam) was driving home from a speaking engagement when the thought hit me, I should whisk Bill away for a surprise. It was Sunday so I knew he would be at church leading the evening service when I got home. The plan formulated so fast, it amazed me. I called a friend to ask if she could watch the kids overnight. I made a hotel reservation with a free room coupon I had. When I got home, I put on an outfit that I knew Bill really liked, and I wrote down on a 3x5 card some of the more interesting places we had made love and included an invitation for Bill to go away with me.

As I walked into church, Bill was on his way to the platform to deliver the message for the night. I caught him and placed the card in his shirt pocket.

Well, I (Bill) thought Pam had just given me an announcement that I was supposed to read to the congregation. I took a quick look at it, and my eyes grew real big. All I could get out of my mouth was, "Ohhhh!" and I immediately put the card back in my pocket.

Bill didn't read the note out loud, but he did deliver the shortest sermon in recorded history.

Just recently, I (Bill) have been praying about how to help Pam with a struggle she has had most of her life. She admits to the struggle, so I know she doesn't mind if I talk about it. She is the oldest daughter of an unpredictable, alcoholic father. As a result, she has a nagging fear that she is going to fail. She could never quite get it right with her father because he was always changing the rules, making it impossible to consistently succeed with him. Intellectually, she knows she has accomplished a lot, and though she recognizes the achievements, the fear keeps coming to the surface at inopportune times.

As I am writing this chapter, I have a strong sense that the next time she says she is afraid she is going to fail, it will help if I say to her, "You can't be a failure because you have won my heart!" What do you think? I doubt it will instantly convince her she can't fail, but I think it might become a good part of our relationship.

(Note from Pam: Bill even flirts with me and encourages me as we write this book together. Yes, it works! *Smooth, Bill. Thanks Holy Spirit for inspiring him.*)

PRACTICE THE PRESENCE

Ask the Holy Spirit to give you ideas this week for encouraging your spouse. As possibilities jump out at you, write them down. Look especially for:

- Songs, billboards, bumper stickers, Bible verses, and greeting cards
- Acts of kindness for you to do for your spouse
- The Spirit's whisper of something unique to say to your lover.

DECODING DELIGHT:
Enjoy a little bit of fun together

Decoder Moments

On page 55 in *The Marriage Code,* we encouraged you to finish the following two statements. Write down how you would finish them and then share them with your spouse:

When you touch me, I feel as if I could…

My favorite way you touch me is…

Husbands, on page 56 we encouraged you to "create a way to tell your wife she is a positive difference maker and that your life (or the family, the community, the church, the world) is better for having her in it." Write out below your strategy for how you plan to do this:

Wives, on page 56 we encouraged you to "create a way to tell your husband you believe in him (his talents, gifts, strength, love, responsibility, character)." Write out below how you plan to communicate that with him:

Work through the Decoder Moment on pages 71-73 that helps you discover your unique abilities, then fill in the two statements below:

I believe my unique abilities are...

I believe my spouse's unique abilities are...

GETTING READY FOR DINNER
Preparation for Your Dinner and Dialogue Assignment

Write out your thoughts on the following:

When I look at you, the unique strength I see is…

What I most appreciate about this strength is…

Then pray for wisdom as you discuss the following questions in response to your spouse's insight:

What can I do that encourages you in this area?

What is the kindest thing I have ever said? Done?

How does the way I touch you impact your area of strength and uniqueness?

LOVE LETTER

Choose one of the prompts below to write a love letter to your spouse:

- The song that best describes our relationship is…
- The reasons I love this song are…

Encouragement means to be called alongside to bring out the best in another individual.

- The ways you have brought out the best in me are…
- The ways I hope to bring out the best in you are…

Chapter 4

Recreation

"The fruit of the Spirit is...patience..."

How can we move so quickly from best friends at the wedding altar into enemies? Divorce court stories show the decline. One man said:

> Ever since we got married, my wife has tried to change me. She got me to exercise daily, have a much better diet, stop drinking, smoking. She taught me how to dress well, enjoy the fine arts, gourmet cooking, classical music and how to invest in the stock market. Now I want a divorce, because I'm so improved, she just isn't good enough for me.

One woman said:

> I was applying for a job in a Florida lemon grove, and the interviewer thought I seemed way too qualified for the job.
>
> "Look, Miss," said the foreman, "have you any actual experience in picking lemons?"
>
> "Well, as a matter of fact, yes!" I replied. "I've been divorced three times."

If a relationship can erode, then that also means a couple can choose *to build* a friendship too—and God's Spirit can help.

QUICK REVIEW

The main point of chapter 4 is that "successful couples have 'a mutual respect for and enjoyment of each other's company.'"[3] In other words, secure and successful couples make their friendship one of their highest priorities. A friendship between a husband and wife that builds an atmosphere of security and success has the following characteristics: They play together, they laugh together, they influence each other equally, they get to know each other, and they find their pace as a couple.

STRATEGIC PRAYER

As you study this chapter, pray this prayer each day this week to focus your heart on your friendship with your mate.

> Lord, I know that I was created to be productive. I was fearfully and wonderfully made by You when I was in the womb (Psalm 139:14). You have given me talents and unique abilities that are designed to be fully utilized. I am Your workmanship, created in Christ Jesus for good works that I should walk in them (Ephesians 2:10). My spouse is equally talented and I can help him or her succeed without sacrificing my own success (Hebrews 10:24-25). I also realize it is always good to do the right thing and that no true success can come from doing the wrong thing (1 Peter 2:15). I therefore commit to do good to my spouse by encouraging him or her daily as long as it is called today (Hebrews 3:13). Jesus, help my spouse feel as loved as possible today! Amen.

CODE SEARCH:
A Look in the Word

Read Proverbs 5:18-19

> May your fountain be blessed,
> and may you rejoice in the wife of your youth.

A loving doe, a graceful deer—
> may her breasts satisfy you always,
> may you ever be captivated by her love.

In what ways does the Bible describe the relationship between a husband and wife as a fun relationship?

Read Romans 8:5-6

> Those who live according to the sinful nature have their minds set on what that nature desires; but those who live in accordance with the Spirit have their minds set on what the Spirit desires. The mind of sinful man is death, but the mind controlled by the Spirit is life and peace.

How do people think who are living according to the sinful nature?

In contrast, how do people think who are living according to the Spirit?

Read Galatians 5:16-21

> So I say, live by the Spirit, and you will not gratify the desires of the sinful nature. For the sinful nature desires what is contrary to the Spirit, and the Spirit what is contrary to the sinful nature. They are in conflict with each other, so that you do not do what you want. But if you are led by the Spirit, you are not under law.
>
> The acts of the sinful nature are obvious: sexual immorality, impurity and debauchery; idolatry and witchcraft; hatred, discord, jealousy, fits of rage, selfish ambition, dissensions, factions and envy; drunkenness, orgies, and the like. I warn you, as I did before, that those who live like this will not inherit the kingdom of God.

What characteristics can you expect to see in the life of someone who is not filled with the Holy Spirit?

Which of these characteristics often show up in many marriages?

Which have shown up in *your* marriage?

Read Galatians 5:22-23

> But the fruit of the Spirit is love, joy, peace, patience, kindness, goodness, faithfulness, gentleness and self-control. Against such things there is no law.

What characteristics can you expect to see in your life when you are filled with the Holy Spirit?

How will these characteristics make it easier to build a marriage that is above the line of trust?

Which fruit, if you exercised it regularly through Spirit-filled living, do you think would make the most positive impact on your marriage?

GOD'S HELP TO GET ABOVE THE LINE:
Mimic the Way the Holy Spirit Thinks

Loving your spouse is a dynamic, fascinating, frustrating, and remarkably rewarding experience. It is also the challenge of your life. Developing a relationship that operates above the line, where security and success are common, is a cooperative venture between you and the Holy Spirit. It is the Spirit's job to soften our hearts and empower us to truly love. It is our job to be cooperative. One of the ways to train ourselves to have a cooperative attitude is to mimic the way the Spirit approaches life.

We know, of course, that we can never do what the Holy Spirit does, but we can focus our thoughts and actions to give Him wider access to our lives. Mimicking the Spirit is different than trying to be the Spirit. To mimic means you will do what you believe the Spirit would do in the situation you are in with the hope that He will get actively involved in your situation.

So, how do you mimic the Spirit?

One way is to choose to think the way the Spirit thinks. The way the Spirit thinks is revealed in the Bible. As you read, hear, and study the Bible, you will become aware of the Spirit's perspective on life and love. You can then choose to adopt the same perspective. Read the following verses and make notes about how the Holy Spirit thinks:

Proverbs 15:26—"The LORD detests the thoughts of the wicked, but those of the pure are pleasing to him."

Colossians 3:2—"Set your minds on things above, not on earthly things."

Romans 8:28—"And we know that in all things God works for the good of those who love him, who have been called according to his purpose."

Romans 14:13—"Therefore let us stop passing judgment on one another. Instead, make up your mind not to put any stumbling block or obstacle in your brother's way."

Galatians 4:6-7—"Because you are sons, God sent the Spirit of his Son into our hearts, the Spirit who calls out, 'Abba, Father.' So you are no longer a slave, but a son; and since you are a son, God has made you also an heir."

Galatians 5:17—"For the sinful nature desires what is contrary to the Spirit, and the Spirit what is contrary to the sinful nature. They are in conflict with each other, so that you do not do what you want."

Philippians 4:8—"Finally, brothers, whatever is true, whatever is noble, whatever is right, whatever is pure, whatever is lovely, whatever is admirable—if anything is excellent or praiseworthy—think about such things."

Galatians 6:7-8—"Do not be deceived: God cannot be mocked. A man reaps what he sows. The one who sows to please his sinful nature, from that nature will reap destruction; the one who sows to please the Spirit, from the Spirit will reap eternal life."

What did you learn about choosing to think the way the Holy Spirit thinks that might improve your marriage?

There are times I (Pam) want to yell, scream, belittle, pout, get revenge, or manipulate, but the summer before my wedding day, I did a study on the person of the Holy Spirit, and never once did I see those actions or attitudes in Him. So when Bill and I were newly-weds and we had so many adjustments to make, I might try to yell or pout or manipulate, but it made me feel so miserable and it was so counterproductive that I quickly apologized to God and Bill for my behavior. I discovered that I liked myself and my life better when I didn't have to go through all the drama and then end up apologizing, so I just learned to skip those steps and went straight to the question, "What would the Spirit do?" I am definitely not perfect, but I am a much improved model compared to the drama queen Bill married.

Sometimes choosing to mimic the Spirit is the consistent ability to utter a prayer under your breath over and over, moment by moment. Once in our marriage, Pam made a business decision that affected everything in our life: our finances, our schedule, our family rhythm—and mostly my (Bill's) schedule. I had a deep underlying anger. We talked the issue out. I forgave Pam, but I found that I was still short-tempered toward her, fearful of what might be around the corner.

I decided I would pray with the same regularity as I breathed. I would pray, "Lord, You love Pam. Show me how to love her." Then God would encourage me to say something kind or do something kind or sometimes God would just tell me to walk away and be silent. That Spirit-led prayer to be like the Spirit helped us through a long and difficult few years as we all adjusted to the consequences of Pam's decision.

God is working everything out for good, and now years later, I can even see some wisdom in Pam's decision. Often we cannot see all the details of a situation, and we definitely cannot discern a person's motives. But God sees all that, so when we are tuned in to the Spirit and mimic His actions, we are more likely to treat people appropriately, especially when we might be prone to being reactionary or emotional. Mimicking the Spirit can calm a situation and create an environment for peacemaking.

If I would have reacted in my flesh, I could have destroyed all the good God had built into our relationship. Responding in the Spirit created an atmosphere of grace in our home, and Pam's heart was drawn to me as I extended the kind of mercy, grace, forgiveness, and tenderness that God did toward her.

PRACTICE THE PRESENCE

In the chart below, make a list of the commitments you have at work this week. Next to each commitment, describe what the Holy Spirit thinks about this responsibility of yours. You can start by using thoughts from the verses you studied above. As you grow in this skill, you can use thoughts from verses you encounter in your personal growth.

My commitments at work this week:	What the Holy Spirit thinks about this commitment:

Next make a list of the activities you are going to enjoy with your spouse this week and describe what the Holy Spirit thinks about these activities.

Activities I will enjoy with my spouse:	What the Holy Spirit thinks about these activities:

DECODING DELIGHT:
Enjoy a little bit of fun together

Decoder Moments

On pages 83-85 of *The Marriage Code*, we encourage you to fill out your dating preferences. Share your answers with your spouse and decide together on a dating routine for your relationship

On pages 95-97, we encourage you to fill out your preferences when it comes to the pace of life. Share your answers with your spouse and discuss what pace you think is best for your relationship.

GETTING READY FOR DINNER
Preparation for Your Dinner and Dialogue Assignment

On page 98, we encourage you to "share what a 'real day off' might look like." Take a few moments here to describe your ideal day off as you prepare to present this to your spouse.

LOVE LETTER

Write a love letter to your mate this week with the following information:

- The things I love to do with you are…
- The times I have had the most fun with you are…
- The favorite thing I know about you is…
- The thing I know about you that I think most people don't know is…

Chapter 5

Resolving Conflicts

"The fruit of the Spirit is...peace..."

It seems so easy to fall into conflict and so hard to work our way through it. These refrigerator magnet-type comments reveal the dilemmas couples often find themselves in:

- When a husband's words are sharp, it may be from trying to get them in edgeways.

- If your dog is barking at the back door and your wife is yelling at the front door, who do you let in first? The dog—you know he'll shut up when he comes in.

- I love being married. It's so great to find that one special person you want to annoy for the rest of your life.

- I just got back from a pleasure trip—I drove my wife to the airport.

- "Bigamy is having one wife too many. Monogamy is the same" (Oscar Wilde).

But we don't have to settle for a life of conflict. We can actually use our disagreements to build into our relationship. With God's help, an argument can become an opportunity to morph misery into the magnificent.

QUICK REVIEW

The main point of chapter 5 is that conflict is an ordinary part of every intimate relationship. Conflict, however, can be resolved so that it brings value to your relationship. To maximize the value of your conflicts you are encouraged to recognize the triggers that bring tension to the surface and choose a conflict resolution style (the planned approach, the spontaneous approach, or the delayed approach) that works for you as a couple.

We also introduced you to a check list that can help you SOLVE the issues you face:

- *Seek God together.* Pray together and ask God to give you wisdom to work through the issue.
- *Open the conversation.* Decide who is going to share first.
- *Look deeper.* After both of you have shared sufficiently, ask the question, "What do you think the real issue is?"
- *Verify options.* Once you have identified the real issue, discuss possible solutions.
- *Evolve into the answer.* Be patient as some solutions take time, and there are some challenges in life that don't actually have solutions (e.g., a special needs child).

STRATEGIC PRAYER

As you study this chapter, pray this prayer each day this week to focus your heart to make conflict work for you rather than against you.

Dear Lord, as my God and Creator, You know the end of everything in my life from the beginning. Your purposes will always stand, and You will do what pleases You (Isaiah 46:10). You work out everything in conformity with the purpose of Your will and never need to ask anyone for advice or wisdom (Ephesians 1:11). I believe that You have committed to instruct me and teach me in the way I should go (Psalm

32:8). As a result, I know that all things will work together for good in my life because I love You and have been called according to Your purpose (Romans 8:28). It is in my best interests to wait on You when there is not clear direction because You exalt those who wait on You (Psalm 37:34). I can trust that You will lead me by Your Spirit because I am Your child (Romans 8:14). Since Your Spirit lives in me, I have the ability to wait patiently (Romans 8:25) and to bear with the one I love while You do Your work (Ephesians 4:2), and I can grow in my personal life each and every day of my life (1 Peter 2:1-3). Amen.

CODE SEARCH:
A Look in the Word

Read Psalm 34:14

> Turn from evil and do good;
>> seek peace and pursue it.

Read 1 Peter 3:10-11

> For,
>> "Whoever would love life
>>> and see good days
>> must keep his tongue from evil
>>> and his lips from deceitful speech.
>> He must turn from evil and do good;
>>> he must seek peace and pursue it."

How do these verses relate to conflict in your relationship?

How can you seek peace when you are upset with the other person?

Read Romans 13:12

> The night is nearly over; the day is almost here. So let us put
> aside the deeds of darkness and put on the armor of light.

Many times in Scripture we are instructed to "get dressed." When
we take the "small" steps of getting dressed, God takes the "big" step
of clothing us in the power of the Holy Spirit. With what are we to
clothe ourselves in Romans 13:12?

How do you think you can do this in your everyday life?

Read Ephesians 6:11-17

> Finally, be strong in the Lord and in his mighty power. Put on
> the full armor of God so that you can take your stand against
> the devil's schemes. For our struggle is not against flesh and
> blood, but against the rulers, against the authorities, against
> the powers of this dark world and against the spiritual forces

of evil in the heavenly realms. Therefore put on the full armor of God, so that when the day of evil comes, you may be able to stand your ground, and after you have done everything, to stand. Stand firm then, with the belt of truth buckled around your waist, with the breastplate of righteousness in place, and with your feet fitted with the readiness that comes from the gospel of peace. In addition to all this, take up the shield of faith, with which you can extinguish all the flaming arrows of the evil one. Take the helmet of salvation and the sword of the Spirit, which is the word of God.

With what are we to clothe ourselves in Ephesians 6:11-17?

How do you think you can do this in your everyday life?

The clothes we are to dress in are described as military gear. How might illustrations of these items of warfare, such as "armor of God," help us in our marriages?

How is it helpful to be protected by God's power rather than by our self-protection mechanisms when it comes to relating with your spouse?

When you are in a disagreement with your mate, what do you usually want to do in the flesh? (check any that apply):

☐ get angry

☐ get even

☐ get away

☐ get your mate as upset as you are

☐ get people involved who are not relationship specialists (such as bartender, manicurist, beautician, or dysfunctional family members)

☐ get kids to take sides

Instead, the Spirit can help you get to the heart of the matter.

Read Romans 8:37-39

No, in all these things we are more than conquerors through him who loved us. For I am convinced that neither death nor life, neither angels nor demons, neither the present nor the future, nor any powers, neither height nor depth, nor anything else in all creation, will be able to separate us from the love of God that is in Christ Jesus our Lord.

How are we described in verse 37 because of the Holy Spirit's work in our lives?

How does it help knowing that Jesus is present in all our conflicts through His Spirit?

Read Ephesians 4:30

> And do not grieve the Holy Spirit of God, with whom you were sealed for the day of redemption.

The word *grieve* means to cause sorrow to or to inflict pain. What do you think it means to grieve the Holy Spirit?

In the context (by looking at the surrounding verses), we are reminded we can grieve the Spirit by activities and attitudes such as: living like the pagans (4:17-19), lying (4:25), being angry (4:26-27), stealing (4:28), cursing (4:29), being bitter (4:31), being unforgiving (4:32), and being sexually immoral (5:3-5). There are many ways to grieve the Spirit, but are there any on this list that you struggle with now or struggled with in your past?

How does confession help us avoid grieving the Spirit?

If you did experience grieving the Spirit, how does it feel after you have confessed it before God and come clean?

What did you learn this week that will help you tune in to the Holy Spirit and better manage or avoid conflict in your marriage?

GOD'S HELP TO GET ABOVE THE LINE:
Relieving Spiritual Stress by the Holy Spirit

We don't think we are telling you anything new when we say that marriage is a battleground. We don't mean to say that you are always fighting (although it may feel like it to some of you). We do, however, recognize that there is spiritual stress on your relationship, and unhealthy patterns from the families you grew up in are trying to assert themselves. This is why there are alarms in your relationship. You get upset with each other at ridiculous times. You get afraid or stubborn, even though you know there is no need to do so. You say or do hurtful things only to wonder later why you reacted that way to the person you love the most.

One of the reasons is spiritual stress. Satan and his cohorts do not want your marriage to thrive. He knows your love is a great picture of the love that exists between Christ and His people. If he can distort your love for each other, he can distort the picture some people have of the gospel. You will, therefore, grow tense with one another for no particular reason. This is one reason many people argue on their way to church or some other spiritual growth activity.

Because of the chaotic homes Pam and I grew up in, we were (and are) highly motivated to become experts in the skills in this chapter. They were our life preservers. The Holy Spirit has been the cord binding us together. If we would have acted in our wisdom, we would have wrecked our love and our life right out of the gate. Instead, we chose to listen to God, especially when we found ourselves in disagreement.

There are two skills you can practice to help minimize the spiritual stress in your home. The first is to *pray out loud*. When you become aware of tension and conflict between the two of you, pray first, then talk. Certainly, not all tension and conflict in your relationship is caused by spiritual forces, but they are one of the causes. Before you venture into solving the problem with your own ingenuity, it is wise to eliminate any possible stress caused by the enemy's lies. It is wise to start here because it is the simplest one to deal with. When conflict begins to surface, pray a prayer similar to the one below under the heading, "Practice the Presence." Often the argument will stop as soon as you pray. This happens when the source of your quarrel is spiritual rather than relational.

The other skill you can practice is to *replace lies with truth*. When conflict arises, you can ask, "Is there an obvious lie affecting our interaction?" This is the playground for demons. John 8:44 tells us that Satan is "the father of lies." This is the weapon he has to use against believers. He lies to us and tries to convince us the lie is true. When we believe the lie, we create a small opening of influence that demons exploit to get us frustrated with one another. As soon as you identify the lie and pronounce the truth, you disarm the influence that is causing the conflict. For instance,

- Your husband may be quieter than usual, and you start thinking he doesn't care. The lie is that he doesn't care. The possible truth is he may be overwhelmed, he may be stressed by work, he may be feeling inadequate, and a host of other possibilities.

The obvious truth is that you do not know the motives of the heart since only God knows this about people.

- Your wife may be irritable, and you can't figure out why. The temptation is to let your imagination run wild with possibilities. The truth is that you don't really know what is going on in her heart, but God does. God can guide her, and He can guide you so that you find a workable solution.

The key is to identify the lie out loud and proclaim the truth that counteracts it. If the conflict between you is based on this lie, it will evaporate, and you can get back to a cohesive partnership quickly.

The other lies that cause alarms to go off come from your family of origin. Family patterns are strong, and they work hard to repeat themselves generation after generation. You learned these patterns during your most impressionable years so they are lodged deep within, and they get triggered by emotional responses. Since the triggers are primarily emotional, they surface in your marriage more than in any other relationship in your life.

The Spirit of God wants to use these triggers to cause growth in your life. It is His job to create the growth; it is your job to cooperate. The way you cooperate is through an honest evaluation of the influence of your family of origin. This is one application of Genesis 2:24, "For this reason a man will leave his father and mother and be united to his wife, and they will become one flesh."

Young couples did not move away from their families for most of history. They shared the same property, the same business, and much of the same social life. The leaving process is really about taking steps to establish a new home based on decisions rather than reactions.

PRACTICE THE PRESENCE

Practice saying this prayer out loud together for five days when you are not in conflict with each other. Then open tense decisions with this prayer before you begin your discussion.

Dear Jesus, we thank You for Your victory on the cross. We know that Your death and resurrection has made us more than conquerors. We, therefore, humbly stand with You and in Your name we command any evil spirits who are around to be quiet and not operate in any way in or around our relationship. We announce that we are a team and that our love is a reflection to the world around us of Your love. We commit our conversation to You now, and we ask that You give us Your power to work together today. Amen.

In preparation for identifying lies and proclaiming the truth that is opposite these lies, work through the following steps:

Step 1: Ask, "What is healthy in my family that I want to incorporate into my life?"

Step 2: Ask, "What is unhealthy in my family that I want to replace with more productive behaviors?"

Step 3: What productive behavior do I want to practice instead of the unhealthy behavior that gets triggered?

Step 4: Ask the Holy Spirit to give you power to accomplish steps 1 through 3.

DECODING DELIGHT:
Enjoy a little bit of fun together

Decoder Moments

On page 104 of *The Marriage Code,* we challenged you to fight boredom in your relationship by describing "one idea you'd like to try, place you'd like to go, or experience you'd like to have that is outside your comfort zone (but not immoral or illegal)." So go ahead and describe it here:

On page 107, we encouraged you to "share one incident from your past (before your wedding day) that still triggers emotions in your marriage." This can be delicate and sensitive, so take time to describe this in writing before you share it. You may even want to write it out on a computer so you can edit it before anyone else gets to see it.

GETTING READY FOR DINNER
Preparation for Your Dinner and Dialogue Assignment

Choose which conflict resolution style you prefer. You may even want to take time to write down why you prefer this approach so you can communicate it clearly. I prefer:

- ☐ *The Planned Approach* (schedule a time to meet to discuss what you are upset about)
- ☐ *The Spontaneous Approach* (deal with issues as they come up)
- ☐ *The Delayed Approach* (take a break for a short time before you work your way through the issue)

LOVE LETTER

Include your thoughts on the following topics in your letter to your lover this week:

- Let me tell you how I have become a stronger person through our disagreements.

- I am committed to win the spiritual battles in our life together because we are a team.

- I want to work through difficult areas with you because I love being with you.

Chapter 6

Intimacy

"The fruit of the Spirit is…faithfulness…"

I n our book *Red Hot Monogamy,* we write that "sex was God's secret a long time before it was Victoria's Secret." God wants us to reclaim the gift. Unfortunately for many couples, this most precious area of love is the source for the greatest contention. The following joke shows how our differences in this area can escalate to the irrational:

> A man walks into his bedroom and sees his wife packing a suitcase. He says, "What are you doing?"
>
> She answers, "I'm moving to Las Vegas. I heard ladies-of-the-night there get paid $400 for doing what I do for you for free."
>
> Later that night, on her way out, the wife walks into the bedroom and sees her husband packing his suitcase.
>
> When she asks him where he's going, he replies, "I'm going to Vegas too. I want to see you live on $800 a year."

You do not have to live this way. There is a better way. God is the creator of the gift of sex, so no one knows better how to develop intimacy than the Spirit. If you tune in to the Spirit, you will be tuned in to how to better love, romance, and enjoy sexual intimacy with your mate.

QUICK REVIEW

The main point of chapter 6 is that sexual love is one of the most fascinating and intricate activities that humans engage in because it is the knitting together of two individuals physically, emotionally, spiritually, and adventurously.

STRATEGIC PRAYER

As you study this chapter, pray this prayer each day this week to focus your heart on the passion in your relationship.

> Jesus, thank You for creating my spouse and me as sexual beings. I commit my body today as an instrument of righteousness (Romans 6:13) so that I can glorify You in my body (1 Corinthians 6:20). Give me strength to fulfill my duty to my spouse in becoming a better lover with each year that we get to spend together. I thank You for giving my spouse's body to me and for giving my body to my spouse so that we might love each other spiritually, emotionally, and physically. I commit myself today to explore my spouse's body in love, and I ask you to keep us from temptation (1 Corinthians 7:1-5). I believe that the world around us will get a better understanding of Your love when we unlock the combination to love and respect one another (Ephesians 5:33). Amen.

CODE SEARCH:
A Look in the Word

Read 1 Corinthians 7:3-6

> The husband should fulfill his marital duty to his wife, and likewise the wife to her husband. The wife's body does not belong to her alone but also to her husband. In the same way, the husband's body does not belong to him alone but also to his wife. Do not deprive each other except by mutual consent and for a time, so that you may devote yourselves to prayer.

Then come together again so that Satan will not tempt you because of your lack of self-control.

Describe the importance of the physical side of your relationship according to this passage.

How are sex and prayer related to one another in this passage?

Read Song of Solomon 4:1-7

How beautiful you are, my darling!
    Oh, how beautiful!
    Your eyes behind your veil are doves.
Your hair is like a flock of goats
    descending from Mount Gilead.
Your teeth are like a flock of sheep just shorn,
    coming up from the washing.
Each has its twin;
    not one of them is alone.
Your lips are like a scarlet ribbon;
    your mouth is lovely.
Your temples behind your veil
    are like the halves of a pomegranate.
Your neck is like the tower of David,
    built with elegance;
on it hang a thousand shields,
    all of them shields of warriors.

Your two breasts are like two fawns,
    like twin fawns of a gazelle
    that browse among the lilies.
Until the day breaks
    and the shadows flee,
I will go to the mountain of myrrh
    and to the hill of incense.
All beautiful you are, my darling;
    there is no flaw in you.

What does Solomon do to increase intimacy with his wife?

Read Song of Solomon 5:10-16

My lover is radiant and ruddy,
    outstanding among ten thousand.
His head is purest gold;
    his hair is wavy
    and black as a raven.
His eyes are like doves
    by the water streams,
washed in milk,
    mounted like jewels.
His cheeks are like beds of spice
    yielding perfume.
His lips are like lilies
    dripping with myrrh.
His arms are rods of gold
    set with chrysolite.
His body is like polished ivory
    decorated with sapphires.

His legs are pillars of marble
   set on bases of pure gold.
His appearance is like Lebanon,
   choice as its cedars.
His mouth is sweetness itself;
   he is altogether lovely.
This is my lover, this my friend,
   O daughters of Jerusalem.

What does Solomon's wife do to increase intimacy with her husband?

Both partners in this biblical book took the time to praise each other head to toe. Write out a list, head to toe, of what you appreciate and find physically attractive in your spouse:

Read Romans 8:9-11

You, however, are controlled not by the sinful nature but by the Spirit, if the Spirit of God lives in you. And if anyone does not have the Spirit of Christ, he does not belong to Christ. But if Christ is in you, your body is dead because of sin, yet your spirit is alive because of righteousness. And if the Spirit of him who raised Jesus from the dead is living in you, he who raised Christ from the dead will also give life to your mortal bodies through his Spirit, who lives in you.

How does the presence of the Holy Spirit in your life affect your body?

Read Ephesians 4:20-24

> You, however, did not come to know Christ that way. Surely
> you heard of him and were taught in him in accordance with
> the truth that is in Jesus. You were taught, with regard to your
> former way of life, to put off your old self, which is being cor-
> rupted by its deceitful desires; to be made new in the attitude
> of your minds; and to put on the new self, created to be like
> God in true righteousness and holiness.

With what are we to clothe ourselves according to these verses? What
are we to take off and what are we to put on?

How do you think you can do this in your everyday life?

How do you think this might positively impact your marriage and
family life?

Read I Corinthians 6:19-20

> Do you not know that your body is a temple of the Holy
> Spirit, who is in you, whom you have received from God?
> You are not your own; you were bought at a price. Therefore
> honor God with your body.

What is the connection between the Holy Spirit and your body?

When you think of the word *honor*, what comes to your mind?

What is one way you can show honor to God and your spouse in your
romantic or sexual life?

GOD'S HELP TO GET ABOVE THE LINE:
Praying Through Scripture

As we have discussed in previous chapters, there is a dynamic interaction between the Holy Spirit and the Word of God. The Spirit uses
the Word to get our attention, guide our steps, and grow us up. Every
step you take, therefore, to apply the Bible to your life in a personal

and practical way has a dramatic impact on you. In addition, pray-ing with your spouse is one of the most effective means for creating intimacy in your relationship. One of the best ways we know to do this is to pray through Scripture. Here are some suggestions for how to effectively pray the Bible over your life:

- Choose verses that apply to your life. The Bible is a very personal book and contains a vast number of promises and instructions for our lives. There are, however, some verses that are historical in nature and apply to specific circum-stances. Caution should be taken in these instances that we don't misapply passages. A good example is Psalm 51 where David writes, "Do not take your Holy Spirit from me." In the Old Testament, the Spirit would come upon people for a specific purpose and then remove Himself. In the New Testament, the Spirit indwells believers and will never be removed from them. This was a very real prayer for David that is no longer necessary in the lives of believers.

- Insert your name (or a personal pronoun) into the verse where it is appropriate (see the examples of how to do this below).

- Pray these verses over your life out loud.

Examples:

Ephesians 1:17—"I keep asking that the God of our Lord Jesus Christ, the glorious Father, may give you [me] the Spirit of wisdom and revelation, so that you [I] may know him better."

Ephesians 4:20-24—"You [I], however, did not come to know Christ that way. Surely you [I] heard of him and were [was] taught in him in accordance with the truth that is in Jesus. You were [I was] taught, with regard to your [my] former way of life, to put off your [my] old self, which is being corrupted by its deceitful desires; to be made new in the attitude of your minds [my mind]; and to put on the new self, created to be like God in true righteousness and holiness."

Ephesians 6:11-17—"[Your name] Put on the full armor of God so that you can take your stand against the devil's schemes. For our struggle is not against flesh and blood, but against the rulers, against the authorities, against the powers of this dark world and against the spiritual forces of evil in the heavenly realms. Therefore [your name] put on the full armor of God, so that when the day of evil comes, you may be able to stand your ground, and after you have done everything, to stand. Stand firm then, with the belt of truth buckled around your waist, with the breastplate of righteousness in place, and with your feet fitted with the readiness that comes from the gospel of peace. In addition to all this, take up the shield of faith, with which you can extinguish all the flaming arrows of the evil one. Take the helmet of salvation and the sword of the Spirit, which is the word of God."

Colossians 3:9-12—"[Your name] Do not lie to each other, since you have taken off your old self with its practices and have put on the new self, which is being renewed in knowledge in the image of its Creator. Here there is no Greek or Jew, circumcised or uncircumcised, barbarian, Scythian, slave or free, but Christ is all, and is in all. Therefore, as [one of] God's chosen people, [your name], holy and dearly loved, clothe yourselves [yourself] with compassion, kindness, humility, gentleness and patience."

Hebrews 4:12—"For the word of God is living and active. Sharper than any double-edged sword, it penetrates even to dividing soul and spirit, joints and marrow; it judges the thoughts and attitudes of the [my] heart."

Ephesians 5:21-33—"[Bill and Pam,] Submit to one another out of reverence for Christ.

"Wives [Pam], submit to your husbands [Bill] as to the Lord. For the husband [Bill] is the [your] head of the wife as Christ is the head of the church, his body, of which he is the Savior. Now as the church submits to Christ, so also wives [Pam] should submit to their husbands [Bill] in everything.

"Husbands [Bill], love your wives [Pam], just as Christ loved the church and gave himself up for her to make her holy, cleansing her by the washing with water through the word, and to present her to himself as a radiant church, without stain or wrinkle or any other blemish, but holy and blameless. In this same way, husbands [Bill] ought to love their wives [Pam] as their own bodies [his own body]. He who loves his wife loves himself. After all, no one ever hated his own body, but he feeds and cares for it, just as Christ does the church—for we are members of his body. "For this reason a man [Bill] will leave his father and mother and be united to his wife [Pam], and the two will become one flesh." This is a profound mystery—but I am talking about Christ and the church. However, each one of you [Bill] also must love his wife [Pam] as he loves himself, and the wife [Pam] must respect her husband [Bill]."

PRACTICE THE PRESENCE

Now it's your turn. Choose one of the passages above and pray it out loud as an individual. Then get together with your spouse and share which passage you prayed for yourself. Choose a passage or two together as a couple to pray over each other and say them out loud as you hold hands. Feel free to pray other Scripture passages of your choosing in this same way.

If you want to take the next step, pray and compliment your mate from head to toe as Solomon and his wife did for each other. Pray and ask God to lead your time of intimacy. Pray and thank God for your spouse silently as you make love. Pray together for each other as you complete your time of intimacy and lie in each other's arms.

For one week, practice asking the Spirit to show you how to love, touch, and romance your mate. Try to respond with immediate obedience. Your prayer might sound something like this: "Lord, please show me how to romance my spouse today," or "Lord, show me when to touch and how to touch my mate today so he (or she) might feel encouraged." The Spirit might lead you to touch and not expect sex; be open to what God is doing. Physical touch and sexual intimacy are powerful tools, so the Spirit may need you to re-earn trust in your mate's eyes, or to learn to touch unconditionally, or to learn to romance in a new way. Be open to listen to what God whispers through the Spirit to you in this precious area.

If there has been a sexual sin in the past (sex outside of marriage or some sexual choice you believe was not in alignment with God's Word), kneel at the foot of your bed with your spouse, ask for forgiveness, and ask God to restore and redeem your love for each other.

Be patient when you are rebuilding a romance. Take your time and keep your mate's needs on the forefront. You might be encouraged by using *Red-Hot Monogamy*, an eight-week guidebook to help you add in spark and sizzle. It will help you build or rebuild intimacy, one week of love at a time.

Remember the power to weave a flourishing intimate life rests in your dependence upon God's Spirit. The word for sex in the Old Testament is *to know*, so the Spirit will seek to help you deeply know your mate. And as you get to know each other's hearts, desires, and needs, your love life will move "above the line" to ecstasy and fulfillment.

DECODING DELIGHT:
Enjoy a little bit of fun together

Decoder Moments

Guys, choose two or three actions that rev your engine the quickest and share those with your wife.

☐ She walks by

- ☐ She gets in the shower
- ☐ She gets out of the shower
- ☐ She winks at you
- ☐ She looks at you with a loving expression
- ☐ She gets undressed
- ☐ She gets dressed
- ☐ She bends forward so you get a peak at her breasts
- ☐ She leans forward and looks back at you
- ☐ She whispers any sexual suggestion
- ☐ She suggests you go out on a date
- ☐ She suggests you stay home

Ladies, choose from the following list your favorite two or three interactions that set a romantic mood and share those with your husband.

- ☐ Listening to you with interest
- ☐ Treating your opinions as if they are important
- ☐ Helping with housework
- ☐ Doing a favor
- ☐ Hugging just because he is happy to see you (especially if it is just a little longer than your normal hugs)
- ☐ Spending time together having fun
- ☐ Finishing a project that is important to you
- ☐ Lowering your stress level
- ☐ Getting you to laugh
- ☐ Giving you time off from the kids to relax
- ☐ Giving an unhurried massage
- ☐ Caressing your body in patient foreplay
- ☐ Playing with the kids and enjoying it

☐ Planning a vacation together

☐ Complimenting you for no particular reason

☐ Saying "I am sorry" when he has made a mistake

☐ Saying no to something else so he can spend time with you

☐ Bragging about you in front of friends

GETTING READY FOR DINNER
Preparation for Your Dinner and Dialogue Assignment

What would you like to use as a code word that says, "I am definitely in the mood to be with you sexually."

Wives—*I will practice the following part of the Respect Combination this week:*

☐ Be adventurous with him.

☐ Be interested in him.

☐ Be proud of him.

I will do this by _____

Husbands—*I will practice the following part of the Love Combination this week:*

☐ Be affirming to her.

☐ Be fascinated with her.

☐ Be interactive with her.

I will do this by _____

LOVE LETTER

Write your lover a letter this week by finishing these statements:

- The things we do that make me feel closer to you are...
- You are most sexy to me when...
- My favorite intimate experience this year has been...

Chapter 7

Activating the Alarms

"The fruit of the Spirit is...joy..."

Sometimes it would be nice if an alarm would help rescue us from ourselves:

> A man rushed to the jewelry counter in the store where I work soon after the doors opened one morning and said he needed a pair of diamond earrings. I showed him a wide selection, and quickly he picked out a pair. When I asked him if he wanted the earrings gift-wrapped, he said, "That'd be great. But can you make it quick? I forgot today was my anniversary, and my wife thinks I'm taking out the trash."

Yes, alarms, though a bit annoying, can be quite useful at times.

In love, one wonders if it might be helpful if we had some kind of alarm that warned us when we are skating on thin ice. As a matter of fact, we do have a helpful alarm—God's Spirit. When you are about to sin in a way that would destroy your marriage, to lash out with destructive words, or to take action without thinking, God's Spirit will give you some warning. Alarms bells and whistles will go off—inner feelings of panic, a nagging sense of impending doom or guilt.

The Holy Spirit in me (Pam) sometimes sounds like, "Run, stupid blond girl, run! Can't you see this will destroy all you hold dear? Girl, wake up!" Bill's inner alarm is a little more subdued, usually a whispered "ah ah ah, caution brother" suffices for him.

When we take actions or have attitudes that threaten to move our marriage "below the line," God in His great mercy sends us internal warnings. Our job is to train ourselves to listen to them.

It has always amazed us how folks get so far off track. It is not unusual for us to have in our office a Christian couple, maybe even Christian leaders, where both spouses are mixed up with sins such as adultery, pornography, gambling, drugs, domestic violence, embezzlement, and transgender and homosexual activities. We often wonder, *Weren't there warning signs?*

There were. One of two things happens before a marriage falls apart: (1) The couple quit listening to or turned off the alarms God sent (quenching and grieving the Spirit), or (2) they never knew how to listen for the alarms in the first place so they were at risk from the moment they said "I do."

We have already talked about how to not quench the Spirit. In this chapter we will work on helping you proactively set up alarms and listen to them in a way that will protect your love.

The other skill you will learn is how to recognize when false alarms go off. One of our friends has a car alarm that is so sensitive that if you sneeze near his car, it sets the thing off. His friends, neighbors, and family never act now when they hear the alarm. No one goes running out of the house in their pj's to see if the car is being stolen. No, it's more likely a cat just walked too near the car, and its tail set the thing off.

I (Pam) am not known for my culinary expertise, so my family just rolls their eyes when they hear the smoke alarm. They know the house isn't burning down. No, Mom's just cooking again.

Learning to not react when false alarms are set off in your heart is just as vital. Both skills—listening to accurate alarms and not responding to false alarms—are important for protecting your love.

QUICK REVIEW

The main point of chapter 7 is that alarms sound in your life when things are not right and joy is being threatened. The alarms go off because something is out of balance or some sensitive area of life has been bruised. Your ability to listen to the alarms is one of the keys to a secure and successful marriage.

STRATEGIC PRAYER

As you study this chapter, pray this prayer each day this week to focus your heart to calm the alarms in your relationship.

> Jesus, thank You that You made it possible for me to choose to walk in newness of life. I, therefore, choose today to set my mind on the things above, not on the things that are on earth. I realize that I have died to the old nature, and my life is hidden with You in God. I choose to consider the members of my earthly body as dead to immorality, impurity, passion, evil desire, and greed. I choose instead to put on the new self who is being renewed to a true knowledge according to Your image (Colossians 3:2-10). Fill me with Your power so that I may be kind and tenderhearted to my spouse. Give me the grace to forgive my spouse just as You also have forgiven me (Ephesians 4:32). Develop in me the self-control that will allow me to say no to my fears as I say yes to You. Amen.

CODE SEARCH:
A Look in the Word

Read 1 Peter 3:7-9

> Husbands, in the same way be considerate as you live with your wives, and treat them with respect as the weaker part-ner and as heirs with you of the gracious gift of life, so that nothing will hinder your prayers. Finally, all of you, live in harmony with one another; be sympathetic, love as brothers, be compassionate and humble. Do not repay evil with evil or insult with insult, but with blessing, because to this you were called so that you may inherit a blessing.

What can husbands do from these verses that will help calm the false alarms in their marriages?

What can "all of you" do to calm these kinds of alarms?

Why do you think not repaying evil for evil but choosing to extend a blessing is a better plan for marriage?

Can you think of a time you gave a blessing when you wanted to repay someone with evil? What was the outcome? How did taking the high road make you feel?

Read Romans 8:13-14

Note the two paradoxes in this passage:

For if you live according to the sinful nature, you will die; but if by the Spirit you put to death the misdeeds of the body, you will live, because those who are led by the Spirit of God are sons of God.

If you live according to _____, you will _____.
If you put to _____ the misdeeds of body, you will _____.

What is the evidence of being a child of God in Romans 8:14?

According to *Romans 8:15-16*, what does the Holy Spirit do for us?

> For you did not receive a spirit that makes you a slave again to fear, but you received the Spirit of sonship. And by him we cry, "Abba, Father." The Spirit himself testifies with our spirit that we are God's children.

According to *Romans 8:26-27*, what does the Holy Spirit do for us?

> In the same way, the Spirit helps us in our weakness. We do not know what we ought to pray for, but the Spirit himself intercedes for us with groans that words cannot express. And he who searches our hearts knows the mind of the Spirit, because the Spirit intercedes for the saints in accordance with God's will.

In *Hebrews 9:14*, we are told that the Holy Spirit is eternal. This means that the Holy Spirit has no beginning point and that He will always exist.

> How much more, then, will the blood of Christ, who through the eternal Spirit offered himself unblemished to God, cleanse our consciences from acts that lead to death, so that we may serve the living God!

Because the Spirit had no beginning, He also has no end. That means God is limitless. Does this fact help you grasp God's ability to help you in your life and in your love? How does it make you feel when you think of God's limitless abilities?

GOD'S HELP TO GET ABOVE THE LINE:
Following the Design of the Holy Spirit

Life Is Meant to Be in Motion

One of the great truths of Christian living is that you have been given spiritual gifts that make you a person of influence. You are naturally a talented person and able to accomplish a lot in life. In addition, there are areas of your life that are supernaturally empowered. When you operate in these areas, God works in a special way in and around you. If you are a gifted teacher, others receive unusual insight when you teach. If you are a gifted administrator, organizational tasks get done with unusual efficiency. If you have the gift of helps, people are greatly encouraged by your work behind the scenes. And so on.

On a personal level, you will gain insight into God's plan for your life as you exercise your gifts. As you serve others, you will discover that much of what you do for others applies to you also. You will become one of the people who benefits from the exercise of your gift.

I (Bill) was talking recently with a man whose gifts are in leadership and exhortation. We talked about business issues and the relationships that help build a healthy career. "It's amazing how much productivity gets lost because of problems at home," he said. "I've noticed in my own home that my wife sets the atmosphere for the whole family." We started talking about the impact of our marriages on our productivity, and he said, "When I get home, I'm going to make it my first goal to help my wife feel secure with me. I bet that will help with everything."

He had just given himself advice that he was confident would work. That's how it works. As you use your gift to help others, God will highlight areas of your relationship that will make a big difference.

The following are some habits you can develop to get yourself ready to hear from God as you serve others with your gifts:

- *Serve others.* Practice different areas of service until you discover where the Holy Spirit works in unusual ways in your life. You can serve in many areas because you are inherently talented. As you serve, however, you will notice some areas that are different from the rest. Over time, you will want to focus on these.

- *Listen to what you share with others.* If God is guiding others through your gifts, He may be leading you also.

- *Ask God to use your times of service to give you direction.*

Choose the Opposite

Inside every believer a war is raging. It's the battle between the "old self" and the "new self." The old self is empowered and directed by our natural human nature, which is selfish and deceptive. The new self is empowered and directed by the Holy Spirit, which is other-centered and relationally skillful. Colossians 3:8-15 lays out the contrast between the old self and the new.

But now you must rid yourselves of all such things as these: anger, rage, malice, slander, and filthy language from your lips. Do not lie to each other, since you have taken off your old self with its practices and have put on the new self, which is being renewed in knowledge in the image of its Creator. Here there is no Greek or Jew, circumcised or uncircumcised, barbarian, Scythian, slave or free, but Christ is all, and is in all.

Therefore, as God's chosen people, holy and dearly loved, clothe yourselves with compassion, kindness, humility, gentleness and patience. Bear with each other and forgive whatever grievances you may have against one another. Forgive as the Lord forgave you. And over all these virtues put on love, which binds them all together in perfect unity.

Let the peace of Christ rule in your hearts, since as members of one body you were called to peace. And be thankful.

From this passage, make a list of the practices of the old self.

Make a list of the practices of the new self.

In your marriage, the Holy Spirit will use the contrast between these two natures to give you guidance. You will notice at times that your spouse is operating according to the old self. He or she may be angry or contentious or fearful or any of a hundred other reactions. As this is happening, the Holy Spirit will prompt you to do the opposite. You will have a strange sense that you should respond to anger with gentleness, argumentativeness with peace, or hurtful words with compassion. It will go against your natural inclinations, and you will probably resist it because it makes you feel vulnerable. When you respond in this way, however, you give the Holy Spirit the opportunity to change your spouse's heart and actions.

You have probably noticed that it does not help to point out your spouse's bad behavior, even when you are right. It will create a fire in your relationship, but not the kind that leads to passion!

Try it and see what happens. Colossians 3 refers to this process as "putting off" clothing and "putting on" clothing. The point is that you have a choice, and the choice is usually irritatingly obvious. Your spouse's negative behavior is like a flashlight that points out the positive behavior the Holy Spirit wants to produce in you.

The following are some habits you can develop to get yourself ready to hear from God as you choose the opposite:

- *Practice delaying your response.* When your spouse responds to you in a negative way, count to five before you say or do anything.

- *Practice the opposite behavior.* Ask yourself, "What is the opposite of this negative behavior?" Rather than react to the negative words or actions of your loved one, choose to be positive and encouraging. Then see what God does. It may not happen immediately, but you certainly won't help the situation if you react negatively.

- *Ask God to use your choice of the opposite behavior to improve your marriage.*

PRACTICE THE PRESENCE

To discover how the Holy Spirit leads in your life through your spiritual gifts, choose two or three areas to serve in over the next few months. Look for short-term commitments so you remain free to explore various options during this evaluation process. As you serve, ask God to show you what areas of service He is willing to bless beyond your natural skills.

To gain proficiency in choosing "new nature" behavior, ask yourself, "What is the reaction in my spouse that I don't like but does not intimidate me?" Look for this reaction this week and choose a response that is the opposite of what you experience. Don't tell your spouse you are doing this, just ask God to use your efforts to make a difference.

DECODING DELIGHT:
Enjoy a little bit of fun together

Decoder Moments

On page 162 of *The Marriage Code*, you are encouraged to discuss the following:

Wife—I think my financial motivational style is:

- ☐ Decision-Maker
- ☐ Inspirer
- ☐ Peacekeeper
- ☐ Policy Holder

Husband—I think my financial motivational style is:

- ☐ Decision-Maker
- ☐ Inspirer
- ☐ Peacekeeper
- ☐ Policy Holder

What are the benefits of these styles in your relationship?

GETTING READY FOR DINNER
Preparation for Your Dinner and Dialogue Assignment

On pages 172-73, you were encouraged to identify a toxic decision you made at some time in your past. Record that decision here:

Choose three different courses of action you can take rather than what you normally do:

Idea 1

Idea 2

Idea 3

Choose one of the ideas and write down two or three ways to practice this new behavior:

Practice Plan 1

Practice Plan 2

Practice Plan 3

Share your plan with your spouse and be prepared to thank your spouse when he or she shares.

Share one way you will choose to value your mate when a false alarm goes off. For example, Pam is a gifted leader so she is decisive. Even when I believe the decision is good, right, and solid, my false alarms of my conservative personality and motivational style may get set off. So I choose to compliment Pam even if I am not yet comfortable with how fast the decision might have been made. On the other hand, when my conservative nature slows Pam down, she has decided to thank me for my wisdom instead of reacting negatively toward me.

Sometimes as we make these conscious decisions, we will "fake a pass" to each other and say, "I am on your team, but this one's hard for me so give me some time to process it. I am 'passing' the decision to you in trust, but my feelings haven't caught up yet."

Talk about a unique way to compliment your mate when his or her style causes you discomfort. See if you can come up with a way to affirm your spouse and also inform your spouse that "Yes, I very much love you, but I am also trying to adjust to you."

LOVE LETTER

In your letter this week, thank your spouse. Consider including these ideas:

- Thank you for loving me through the seasons of our life together.
- Thank you for putting up with the areas of my life that are slow to grow.
- Thank you for giving me grace in the areas of my life that are hard to live with.
- Thank you for being gentle with my fears.

Chapter 8

Golden Goals

"The fruit of the Spirit is...goodness..."

There is such a struggle between contentment and achievement:

A farmer had a wife who nagged him unmercifully. From morning till night, she was always complaining about something. The only time he got any relief was when he was out plowing with his old mule. He tried to plow a lot.

One day his wife brought him lunch in the field. He drove the old mule into the shade, sat on a stump, and began to eat his lunch. Immediately his wife began haranguing him again. Complain, nag, nag—it just went on and on.

All of a sudden the mule lashed out with both hind legs and caught her smack in the back of the head. Killed her on the spot.

At the funeral several days later, the minister noticed something odd. When a woman would approach the old farmer, he would listen for a minute, then nod his head in agreement. But when a man approached him, he would listen for a minute, then shake his head in disagreement. This was so consistent, the minister decided to ask the old farmer about it.

So after the funeral, the minister asked the farmer why he nodded his head and agreed with the women but always shook his head and disagreed with all the men.

The farmer said: "Well, the women would say something about how nice my wife looked or how pretty her dress was, so I'd nod my head."

"And what about the men?" the minister asked.

"They wanted to know if the mule was for sale."

Pushing, nagging, and demanding are habits that erode love. However, Spirit-led goals give life and hope, and are the rich mulch that helps love blossom and grow. As a couple, how can you hear God's voice above all others? How can God move you into a place of blessing so that you are maximized as a team for His ultimate glory?

QUICK REVIEW

The main point of chapter 8 is that your life is going to cost you a small fortune. A couple's ability to decipher the best course of action for each spouse sets them free to stay in love. Competition over the plan for your careers erodes love and shuts the vault of your heart toward each other.

We also encouraged you to fill out a budget that incorporates your financial motivational styles so that you agree more and argue less over money.

STRATEGIC PRAYER

As you study this chapter, pray this prayer each day this week to focus your heart on the financial potential of your relationship.

Lord, I do not need to worry about money because You listen to my prayers and are aware of my life (Philippians 4:6-7; Psalm 32:8). Your love is much more satisfying than the love of money (Luke 16:13). You have said You would add everything I need to my life when I seek You (Matthew 6:33). Contentment is more valuable than prosperity because I brought nothing into this world and I will take nothing out of it (1 Timothy 6:6-8).

I also recognize that the love of money can never make me feel as if I belong because whoever loves money never has enough to make him satisfied (Ecclesiastes 5:10). Therefore, when I set my mind on what I desire, it leads only to death. But when I set my mind on what You desire, You will give me life and peace (Romans 8:5-7). I accept that this will require faith on my part because without faith I cannot please You. I believe that You are there and that You will reward me when I seek You (Hebrews 11:6). Amen.

CODE SEARCH:
A Look in the Word

Read the following verses and write down what you learn about finances:

Matthew 6:21

"For where your treasure is, there your heart will be also."

Philippians 4:19

And my God will meet all your needs according to his glorious riches in Christ Jesus.

1 Corinthians 4:2

Now it is required that those who have been given a trust must prove faithful.

Matthew 6:32-34

> "For the pagans run after all these things, and your heavenly
> Father knows that you need them. But seek first his king-
> dom and his righteousness, and all these things will be given
> to you as well. Therefore do not worry about tomorrow, for
> tomorrow will worry about itself. Each day has enough trouble
> of its own."

The apostle Paul tells us that we are saved by the sanctifying work
of the Spirit. *Sanctify* means to "set apart." In what ways do you think
the Holy Spirit has set you apart?

2 Thessalonians 2:13

> But we ought always to thank God for you, brothers loved by
> the Lord, because from the beginning God chose you to be
> saved through the sanctifying work of the Spirit and through
> belief in the truth.

We see in Acts 8:29 and Acts 13:2 that the Spirit gives clear directions.

Acts 8:29

> The Spirit told Philip, "Go to that chariot and stay near it."

Acts 13:2

> While they were worshiping the Lord and fasting, the Holy

Spirit said, "Set apart for me Barnabas and Saul for the work to which I have called them."

What clear directions has the Holy Spirit given to you in the last few weeks?

2 Corinthians 1:21-22

Now it is God who makes both us and you stand firm in Christ. He anointed us, set his seal of ownership on us, and put his Spirit in our hearts as a deposit, guaranteeing what is to come.

2 Corinthians 5:5

Now it is God who has made us for this very purpose and has given us the Spirit as a deposit, guaranteeing what is to come.

How is the Holy Spirit described in these verses from 2 Corinthians? What is the promise associated with this description of Him?

What in the above verses most encouraged you?

How does what you learned about God being in charge of providing all that you need help you in your marriage?

GOD'S HELP TO GET ABOVE THE LINE:
Making Big Decisions with the Holy Spirit

Most of the decisions you must make in life are relatively minor and ordinary. However, some decisions are far reaching and life changing. They have the power to define your future and affect most areas of your life. When you are faced with these prominent decisions, it is wise to take extra caution.

The skill that God has provided for these big decisions is fasting accompanied by a focus on prayer. Fasting is a voluntary decision to forego food (or something else you love) for a specific time. The reasons for doing so are to:

- deny one of your earthly desires (eating) as an act of personal discipline
- use the time you would normally spend preparing and eating food (or doing the activity you love) to focus on prayer
- heighten your spiritual sensibilities to receive wisdom from God

Since fasting sharpens your spiritual focus, you are more likely to gain insight and direction for any decision that is before you.

We present fasting in this "golden goals" chapter because financial decisions turn into major decisions very quickly in the typical marriage. There are major purchases to be made and often there are major disagreements on the priorities of your budget. As a result, money decisions can get personal and breed dissatisfaction or conflict. Fasting can move the two of you onto the same page as an extension of your relationship with God.

There are some simple guidelines to follow when you decide to fast:

- *Set a specific time that you will fast.* The length of time you fast is not as important as the fact that you fasted. If you are new to this discipline, start with a short period of time (one meal, half a day, one day). As you get accustomed to this discipline, you can choose to fast for longer periods.

- *Choose a specific plan for denying yourself food.* You can skip all meals for a day. You can skip one meal for seven days in a row. You can skip sugar for 40 days and so on. You can skip your favorite TV show in order to spend that time praying. The goal is to deny yourself food (or some other pleasurable activity) to focus on prayer.

- *Drink lots of water.* You do not want to get dehydrated while you are fasting.

- *If fasting from food, come off your fast gently.* Introduce whatever you denied yourself back into your diet slowly. If you are going to engage in an intense fast (days without food), consult your physician and the Campus Crusade for Christ International website devoted to fasting (www.ccci.org/growth/growing-closer-to-god/how-to-fast/index.aspx). If you have any health concerns at all, always consult your physician first before fasting or changing dietary habits.

- *Choose a positive attitude.* Jesus says in Matthew 6:16-18, "When you fast, do not look somber as the hypocrites do, for they disfigure their faces to show men they are fasting. I tell you the truth, they have received their reward in full. But when you fast, put oil on your head and wash your face, so that it will not be obvious to men that you are fasting, but only to your Father, who is unseen; and your Father, who sees what is done in secret, will reward you."

- *Spend the time you would normally use preparing and consuming food to pray.* This is your time to specifically seek God for direction on your current decision. Jesus also says in Matthew 7:7-8, "Ask and it will be given to you; seek and you will find; knock and the door will be opened to you. For everyone who asks receives; he who seeks finds; and to him who knocks, the door will be opened."

- *Accompany your prayer with Bible reading.* Jeremiah 36:5-6 sets the example: "Then Jeremiah told Baruch, 'I am restricted; I cannot go to the LORD's temple. So you go to the house of the LORD on a day of fasting and read to the people from the scroll the words of the LORD that you wrote as I dictated. Read them to all the people of Judah who come in from their towns.'"

- *Journal your discoveries.* As you fast, God will impress verses, thoughts, and plans on your heart. As you record these insights, they form together into a decision you can have confidence in.

Do you (or you and your spouse) have a prominent decision in your life right now or coming in the near future? What is it?

Do you think fasting might help bring clarity or wisdom? What kind of a fast-and-pray plan do you think might work for you?

What insight does this passage provide regarding the attitude that God honors in fasting?

Isaiah 58:3-8

> "'Why have we fasted,' they say,
>   'and you have not seen it?
> Why have we humbled ourselves,
>   and you have not noticed?'
> Yet on the day of your fasting, you do as you please
>   and exploit all your workers.
> Your fasting ends in quarreling and strife,
>   and in striking each other with wicked fists.
> You cannot fast as you do today
>   and expect your voice to be heard on high.
> Is this the kind of fast I have chosen,
>   only a day for a man to humble himself?
> Is it only for bowing one's head like a reed
>   and for lying on sackcloth and ashes?
> Is that what you call a fast,
>   a day acceptable to the LORD?
> Is not this the kind of fasting I have chosen:
>   to loose the chains of injustice
>   and untie the cords of the yoke,
>   to set the oppressed free
>   and break every yoke?
> Is it not to share your food with the hungry
>   and to provide the poor wanderer with shelter—

when you see the naked, to clothe him,
and not to turn away from your own flesh and blood?
Then your light will break forth like the dawn,
and your healing will quickly appear;
then your righteousness will go before you,
and the glory of the LORD will be your rear guard."

Record your insights regarding the attitude that God honors in fasting:

PRACTICE THE PRESENCE

Set a date to create your Motivational Budget (see pp. 200-203 in *The Marriage Code*). Fast one day (or part of the day) during the week you are going to meet. See the guidelines above as you prepare. Break the fast, and then meet to discuss. After you meet, write down your observations.

Was this conversation any different from conversations about finances that you have had in the past?

Was it better or worse?

Why do you think it was either better or worse?

What would you do differently next time you fast?

DECODING DELIGHT:
Enjoy a little bit of fun together

Decoder Moments

Prepare for your discussion with your spouse (see pp. 182-83) by filling in your answers to these questions:

What career step do I want to take *this year*?

How does this step reflect my unique ability? (Is it something God has called me to in my skill set, talent, and passion?)

How does this step match my pace? (Will it speed up our life? If so, for how long? Will it slow down our life? If so, for how long?)

How will this step affect our marriage and family? (Will I gain more time or less time with my mate, children, and extended family?)

What career step do I want to take in *the next five years*?

How does this step reflect my unique ability?

How does this step match my pace in life?

How will this step affect our marriage and family?

On pages 184-85 in *The Marriage Code*, you prioritized a number of statements about your career options. Look over the list and answer the following question:

Which of the statements that you marked is the most important to you? Why?

GETTING READY FOR DINNER
Preparation for Your Dinner and Dialogue Assignment

Few subjects are more emotional in a marriage than money. As you prepare to work through your motivational budget (pp. 201-3), write in the space below any questions or concerns you want to bring up during your discussion:

LOVE LETTER

Begin your letter to your lover this week with the following statements:

- The financial accomplishments I am most proud of in our life are…
- The achievements we have made together that I am most grateful to God for are…

Finish your letter with your thoughts on this statement:

- Thank you for working with me on our finances and our goals. I believe our best years are ahead of us because…

Chapter 9

Expressing Yourself

"The fruit of the Spirit is…gentleness…"

Some of you are wondering about being transparent with your motivational style. You might feel like this man who took a personality assessment at work. His friend asked him if he was going to share the results with his wife. The employee said, "No, that would require me to go home and say, 'Sweetie, I just paid someone $400 to tell me what's wrong with me.' Based on that, considering we've been married 23 years, she might hand me a bill for $798,000."[4]

We love an agreeable environment, but would we really want a partner who was just like us, completely agreeable to everything we thought, said, or desired? We don't think so. We would much prefer to have the unique life partner God planned for us. However, to continue to see and appreciate our mate's unique differences, we need the clarity of the Holy Spirit.

When we go to the optometrist, the doctor has us look through a machine and asks, "Can you see better with this lens…or this one?" That is what the Holy Spirit does; He helps us see our spouse through God's eyes and appreciate him or her as a gift. God's Spirit gives us corrective lenses so we can learn to see the best in our mate and the best of what life has to offer us as a couple.

QUICK REVIEW

The main point of chapter 9 is that your mission is to create a safe house for your relationship. When the environment of your relationship feels safe, you open up and become more vulnerable. When the environment feels tense or perilous, you pull back or create conflict. The goal is to maintain a consistent environment of encouragement and vulnerability where security and success can flourish. You can develop this safe environment through strategic body language, effective tone of voice, and the use of words that RAISE a safety net through:

> *Respect*
>
> *Affirmation*
>
> *"I" statements*
>
> *Sincerity*
>
> *Encouragement*

You were also encouraged to minimize the PAIN in your relationship by avoiding comments that focus on the:

> *Past*
>
> *Accusations*
>
> *Insults and name calling*
>
> *Neglect*

STRATEGIC PRAYER

As you study this chapter, pray this prayer each day this week to focus your heart on communicating with your lover.

> Jesus, I thank You that You know the plans You have for me. They are plans to prosper me and not to harm me, plans to give me hope and a future (Jeremiah 29:11). I believe I can accomplish more in life by being gentle toward my spouse than I can by protecting my heart from being controlled (Psalm

18:35). I also believe it is best for me to be gentle toward my spouse because it helps me fight temptation in my life (Galatians 6:1). The reason I can be gentle is that You are near me (Philippians 4:5) regardless of how my spouse is doing today. As I choose to be gentle, Lord, fill me with Your wisdom so that I might make great decisions, and we can have a satisfying marriage (James 3:13,17). Amen.

CODE SEARCH:
A Look in the Word

Read James 1:19

> My dear brothers, take note of this: Everyone should be quick to listen, slow to speak and slow to become angry.

What is the most important communication skill, according to this verse?

Read Ephesians 4:29

> Do not let any unwholesome talk come out of your mouths, but only what is helpful for building others up according to their needs, that it may benefit those who listen.

What do you think is included in "unwholesome talk"?

How do words build others up?

How do words "benefit those who listen"?

Read John 16:13

> But when he, the Spirit of truth, comes, he will guide you into all truth. He will not speak on his own; he will speak only what he hears, and he will tell you what is yet to come.

In what ways does the Spirit communicate?

Read Hebrews 4:12

> For the word of God is living and active. Sharper than any double-edged sword, it penetrates even to dividing soul and spirit, joints and marrow; it judges the thoughts and attitudes of the heart.

Describe in your own words the relationship between the Holy Spirit and the Word of God.

How does this relationship impact your ability to communicate with your spouse?

GOD'S HELP TO GET ABOVE THE LINE:
Mimicking the Actions of the Holy Spirit

In chapter 4 of this study guide, we introduced the idea of mimicking the way the Holy Spirit thinks. It is one of the ways to train ourselves to have a cooperative attitude toward the work that He is doing in our lives. Another way to develop this cooperative attitude is to mimic the way the Holy Spirit acts. When you are faced with a challenging situation, try these steps:

- Focus on an attribute of the Holy Spirit.
- Ask the Spirit to empower you to apply this attribute in your life.
- Begin taking steps as if you have this power.

Let me give you an example. Pam and I have very different motivation styles. She loves attention and being in charge of decisions. I work best when she accepts me for who I am rather than for what I do. This can be quite a challenge, especially as we work together. I am always looking for a collaborative environment where we encourage each other and put our heads together to discover workable solutions. Pam is intent on creating movement and implementing her ideas (which she believes are vital to our progress). This consistently creates two sensitive scenarios.

The first is based on my conviction that the best solutions come from collaboration. This often feels to Pam as if I am slowing things down and making progress harder than it needs to be. In order for her to keep me in the game and avoid creating an environment of discouragement, she often does the following:

- *Focus on an attribute of the Holy Spirit.* I (Pam) remind myself that the Spirit is a team player, that He uses all parts of the body of Christ to accomplish His will, and that His primary goal is to glorify Jesus, not just get the work done. As Romans 12:2-5 says, "Do not conform any longer to the pattern of this world, but be transformed by the renewing of your mind. Then you will be able to test and approve what God's will is—his good, pleasing and perfect will. For by the grace given me I say to every one of you: Do not think of yourself more highly than you ought, but rather think of yourself with sober judgment, in accordance with the measure of faith God has given you. Just as each of us has one body with many members, and these members do not all have the same function, so in Christ we who are many form one body, and each member belongs to all the others."

- *Ask the Spirit to empower you to apply this attribute in your life.* I then ask the Spirit to give me the grace to adopt a collaborative approach.

- *Begin taking steps as if you have this power.* I then start to ask questions about the upcoming decision rather than give directions. I also discipline myself to listen, really listen, in an effort to gain new insight.

This can be hard for Pam because she is wired for action rather than discussion. Whenever she does this, however, our conversations are much different. If we stick with it, both our hearts soften, we both seem to gain new insight and wisdom, and we grow in our appreciation for one another. We are both profoundly aware that the connection of our hearts is something the Holy Spirit does, but Pam's first steps set the process in motion.

The second is based on Pam's conviction that opportunity ought to be seized when it presents itself. This often triggers a negative reaction in me. I am big on priorities and sticking with clearly revealed direction in life. I also like to focus on one thing until I master it. When we jump on opportunities too fast, I feel as if we are being random and spreading ourselves too thin. The problem with this is that sometimes opportunities do present themselves unexpectedly, and they need to be seized before they disappear. In order to prevent discouraging Pam, I will often do the following:

- *Focus on an attribute of the Holy Spirit.* I remind myself that the Holy Spirit is obedient to the Father's will and that His goal is to glorify Jesus, not just carry out His agenda. Jesus says in John 15:26, "When the Counselor comes, whom I will send to you from the Father, the Spirit of truth who goes out from the Father, he will testify about me."

- *Ask the Spirit to empower you to apply this attribute in your life.* I then ask the Spirit to give me the grace to pursue this opportunity before I have all the information I think I need.

- *Begin taking steps as if you have this power.* I then start to take action. I will transfer money to the project, go to meetings where we are negotiating how to make the idea work, and accept tasks that will help move the project forward.

As I do this, I am often surprised at how well the new opportunity develops. Many of our writing projects developed this way. Our oldest son's college opportunity developed this way. The discovery of our favorite romantic restaurant in the country revealed itself this way. I am convinced these discoveries were all brought to us by the Holy Spirit, but they didn't manifest themselves until I decided to be cooperative with the way God works in Pam's life.

PRACTICE THE PRESENCE

Now you try it. Describe a situation in your life that you would like the Spirit's help with. (It may be a situation coming in the near future or it may be a scenario that has played itself out over and over in your love relationship.)

Choose an attribute of the Holy Spirit that would help resolve this situation (you may choose more than one).

Ask the Holy Spirit to empower you to demonstrate this attribute. Describe two or three steps you can take that would demonstrate this attribute in your life.

DECODING DELIGHT:
Enjoy a little bit of fun together

Decoder Moments
In your own words describe the type of body language and tone of

voice that make you feel most comfortable when you are with your spouse.

GETTING READY FOR DINNER
Preparation for Your Dinner and Dialogue Assignment

In personal conversation,

What hand motions encourage you? What hand motions make you uncomfortable?

How close do you like others to lean toward you?

How does it affect you when the other person crosses arms or legs?

What type of physical contact makes you comfortable? Makes you uncomfortable?

What type of eye contact makes you comfortable? Makes you uncomfortable?

What tone of voice helps you relax? What tone of voice causes stress for you?

Mark the questions below that you would like to discuss with your spouse (from *The Marriage Code,* pp. 227-28):

- ☐ How have your dreams in life changed over the past five years?
- ☐ What has been your favorite adventure during the past year?
- ☐ If you could travel to anyplace in the world, where would you want to go and why?
- ☐ If you described your life right now as a sporting event, what event would it be? Why?

☐ If you described your life right now as a song, what title would that song have? Why?

☐ If you could spend an entire day with anyone in the world, who would you want to spend the day with? What would you want to ask that person?

LOVE LETTER

Write a love letter to your spouse based on the ways to RAISE a safety net in your love:

- The thing I **R**espect most about you is...
- The trait I want to **A**ffirm in you is...
- The thing **I** love the most in you is...
- The trait in you I **S**incerely trust is...
- I want to **E**ncourage you to...

Chapter 10

Accessing the Marriage Code

"The fruit of the Spirit is...self-control."

We can get a little stubborn, and want our own way, and we'll use all means to get our point across:

> A man and his wife were having an argument about who should brew the coffee each morning.
>
> "You should do it because you get up first," the wife said, "and then we don't have to wait as long to get our coffee."
>
> "You are in charge of cooking around here, and you should do it because that's your job," the husband said. "I can just wait for my coffee."
>
> "No, you should do it, and besides, it's in the Bible that the man should do the coffee."
>
> "I can't believe that. Show me."
>
> So she fetched a Bible and opened the New Testament and showed him at the top of several pages that it indeed says... HEBREWS.

Instead of contention, it is so much better to live in cooperation with each other and to respond to each other with love, as the Spirit intended. How is maintaining unity and the red-hot love that results possible day to day?

QUICK REVIEW

The main point of chapter 10 is that in all our years of teaching, equipping, and counseling, the one skill that we have seen as the most vital is the desire to want a marriage that is "above the line." No one can make you want a better marriage; that is a choice only you can make. But we do know an easier way to gain this desire. Ask God. God created marriage, so He has the access codes to both your hearts.

STRATEGIC PRAYER

As you study this chapter, we encourage you to pray these two prayers from chapter 10 in *The Marriage Code* every day this week:

Husband's prayer: Lord, You know my desire to succeed. Please help me view success from Your vantage point. Give me the ability to succeed in life through Your power, not my own. Most importantly, help me succeed with my wife and give me ideas and the wisdom to help her feel more secure in life and love.

Wife's prayer: Lord, You know my desire to feel secure. Please help me view You as my safety net, my shield, my protector and provider. As I rest in my security in You, help me feel secure in my husband's love. Give me the ability to succeed in life through Your power not my own. Most importantly, help me function from a place of security so I can be a better helpmate to my husband and his success.

CODE SEARCH:
A Look in the Word

Read Galatians 4:4-7

But when the time had fully come, God sent his Son, born of a woman, born under law, to redeem those under law, that we might receive the full rights of sons. Because you are sons, God sent the Spirit of his Son into our hearts, the Spirit who calls out, "Abba, Father." So you are no longer a slave, but a son; and since you are a son, God has made you also an heir.

Describe the results of having the Holy Spirit:

Read 1 Corinthians 12:13

For we were all baptized by one Spirit into one body—whether Jews or Greeks, slave or free—and we were all given the one Spirit to drink.

This verse tells us that we have been baptized into the body of Christ. *Baptize* means to "dip, immerse, submerge." Write out in your own words what it means to be immersed in Christ.

How are you fully identifying with Christ through God's Spirit?

If you have never been physically baptized to identify yourself publically as a Christian, ask God when He would like you to also take this step. Sometimes couples decide to be baptized together as a declaration that they each have made the decision to follow Christ and now they will together follow Him. Talk to your pastor for more information.

Read John 3:3-7

> In reply Jesus declared, "I tell you the truth, no one can see the kingdom of God unless he is born again."
>
> "How can a man be born when he is old?" Nicodemus asked. "Surely he cannot enter a second time into his mother's womb to be born!"
>
> Jesus answered, "I tell you the truth, no one can enter the kingdom of God unless he is born of water and the Spirit. Flesh gives birth to flesh, but the Spirit gives birth to spirit. You should not be surprised at my saying, 'You must be born again.'"

Describe in your own words the importance of the Holy Spirit in your Christian walk.

Read Titus 3:4-7

> But when the kindness and love of God our Savior appeared, he saved us, not because of righteous things we had done, but because of his mercy. He saved us through the washing of rebirth and renewal by the Holy Spirit, whom he poured out on us generously through Jesus Christ our Savior, so that, having been justified by his grace, we might become heirs having the hope of eternal life.

According to this passage, what does the Holy Spirit do for us?

What are the results of this work in our lives?

Read John 3:8

> "The wind blows wherever it pleases. You hear its sound, but
> you cannot tell where it comes from or where it is going. So
> it is with everyone born of the Spirit."

What is the Holy Spirit compared to in this verse? In your own words,
what does this say about the Spirit?

Read John 4:13-14

> Jesus answered, "Everyone who drinks this water will be thirsty
> again, but whoever drinks the water I give him will never

> thirst. Indeed, the water I give him will become in him a
> spring of water welling up to eternal life."

What is the Holy Spirit compared to in this passage? In your own
words, what does this say about the Spirit?

GOD'S HELP TO GET ABOVE THE LINE:
Growing in the Power of the Holy Spirit

The Process of Growth

We are committed to the notion that God makes His will obvious
at the right time in our lives. Verses such as, "Do not be foolish but
understand what the will of the Lord is" (Ephesians 5:17) suggest that
God has dedicated Himself to give us wisdom, direction, and specific
instructions as we take the journey of our lives. He does not, however,
lead us as a parent would a small child. If God wanted us to remain
immature throughout our lives, He would simply give us instructions
to do this or do that. Instead, He wants us to fully participate as adults.
To accomplish this, He has created an interactive relationship with
Him. This interactive process includes biblical input, worship, service
according to our gifts, and choosing the opposite.

The Word Is Alive

Hebrews 4:12 tells us, "For the word of God is living and active.
Sharper than any double-edged sword, it penetrates even to dividing
soul and spirit, joints and marrow; it judges the thoughts and attitudes of the heart." Ephesians 6:17 informs us that the Word of God
is "the sword of the Spirit." This means that the Holy Spirit utilizes
the words of the Bible to guide our steps.

As you spend time reading and hearing the Bible, you will notice that some verses jump off the page at you. Some of these verses help you feel better about yourself and about life. Others will disturb you and make you aware of some area of your life that God wants to change. As you pay attention to these verses, God interactively leads you toward His plan for you.

For instance, I (Bill) recently made a significant career transition. For a man, this is often one of the hardest transitions because men are highly motivated by success. I was good at what I did and loved going to work. I also love what I am doing now, but the change required a high degree of learning and a whole new approach to career building. I was nervous about the process and was seeking confirmation from God. During this search, I read Psalm 32:8-9.

> I will instruct you and teach you in the way you should go;
>> I will counsel you and watch over you.
> Do not be like the horse or the mule,
>> which have no understanding
> but must be controlled by bit and bridle
>> or they will not come to you.

As soon as I read it, two thoughts flooded my mind. The first was, *Jesus has taken a personal interest in leading me through this transition in my life.* The second was, *I am stubborn and I need to give in to the change. I can either cooperate with this change and get through it relatively easily, or I can fight the change and experience a long year.*

I (Pam) was sitting in church one day during this transitional period in our life. Right in the middle of the sermon, the words, *This is the way, walk in it*, became vibrant in my mind. I cannot say that I heard them out loud, but the words impacted me as if God had said them. I had heard that passage many times before, but it had never affected me like this. I knew that God was using His Word to give me confidence in the midst of this transition.

It won't happen every day or every week or maybe even every year. But periodically the Bible will come alive for you. You may be reading it, hearing it, studying it with friends, listening to it on the radio, or you may hear a phrase that sparks a verse you have committed to memory. You don't have to go looking for it. You simply need to stay consistent in exposing yourself to God's Word. We encourage you to have a daily plan for growth. Include the following in your plan:

The time of day I like best to spend with God is:

My plan for reading or studying the Bible is:

The place I like to be when I spend time with God in study and prayer is:

How I will share with my mate what I am learning from God will be:

The Spirit of God will direct your exposure to the Bible to guide your decisions and commitments to line up with His will. Keep in mind that God wants to lead you more than you want to be led. He will make it obvious so that you don't have to wonder or worry.

You can develop certain habits to get yourself ready to hear from God in His Word:

- Interact with the Bible in a variety of ways. Set a simple plan for reading, hearing, studying, memorizing, and meditating on the Word of God.

- Ask God to use His Word to direct your life.

- Keep track of the times that God's Word becomes vibrant for you. Write down the verses and your reaction each time God uses the Bible to give you clear directions.

- "Give God permission" to cause verses to jump off the pages of Scripture as often or as seldom as He wants. God does not need your permission for anything, but this helps shape your attitude so that you do not get disappointed if He doesn't respond as often as you would like.

Worship Tunes You In

> You are awesome, O God, in your sanctuary;
> > the God of Israel gives power and strength to his people.
> Praise be to God!
> > (Psalm 68:35)

One of the biggest challenges in figuring out how God wants to work in our lives is getting our eyes off ourselves. By nature, we are self-centered and self-absorbed. Marriage, however, is by nature other-centered. Worship gives you something bigger than you and bigger than life to focus on. The more you worship, the more other-centered you become.

As a result, God will periodically give you direction in the midst of worship. You may be listening to a song, and the answer to your question comes into focus. You may be singing, and a decision suddenly becomes clear. You may be expressing yourself in prayer, and the next step in your journey reveals itself. This happens because God trusts people who have their eyes off themselves.

I (Bill) was recently in Israel visiting many of the sites where Jesus carried on His earthly ministry. We were in the city of Capernaum, the home base from which Jesus operated. This was a strategic city because people would stay there on their travels between Damascus and Jerusalem. People from all over the then-known world would congregate there to rest and stock up on supplies. When Jesus performed a miracle, word would spread quickly because travelers would take the news either to Jerusalem or to Damascus.

I took some time to pray and honor God for the wise way He launched the gospel. As I did, the realization hit me that Jesus had prepared the disciples for exactly what He wanted them to do. Seven of the disciples were from Capernaum, so they had been exposed to the nations of the world all their life. When Jesus announced to them, "make disciples of all nations," they had a mental picture of what that meant. Then I realized that God has prepared me for what He wants me to do in life. He has been taking steps my whole life to get me ready for His plan.

You can develop certain habits to get yourself ready to hear from God in worship:

- Attend church regularly so you can participate in a corporate worship experience. Sing during the singing (no matter how you sing), follow the worship leader's instructions, and focus on the words that are being used to honor God.

- Practice telling God in your personal prayer time how great He is. Review His characteristics and use what is true about Him to honor Him with your words.

- Play worship music while you accomplish everyday tasks.

- Ask God to use your times of worship to give you direction in life.

PRACTICE THE PRESENCE

Ask God to cause something from the Bible to stand out to you this week. Set a regular time to read from the Bible each day. If you don't have a routine set up, begin reading in the book of John or perhaps read one psalm and one proverb each day. As you do so, write down any verses that seem more vibrant to you than others. Then ask God, "What do You want me to do in response to these verses?"

Play worship music at home or in your car each day this week. A Christian bookstore is one place to discover good music with scriptural themes in the style of music you prefer. As you listen, ask God to use thoughts from the songs to give direction to your life.

DECODING DELIGHT:
Enjoy a little bit of fun together

Decoder Moments

Describe the time in your life when you began a personal relationship with Jesus. If you have never done so, share your story of faith with your spouse and family or your friendship circle.

On your dinner date this week, discuss the following: "I would like us to get to know God better this year by adding this to our life..." (check one or two as a priority):

- ☐ Read the Bible together
- ☐ Have separate quiet times but set up a time each day (or each week) to share what we are learning
- ☐ Join a couple's small group Bible study
- ☐ Pray together (What time? In the morning over coffee? At night in bed? Over meals?)
- ☐ Share our story of love and faith with other couples we know
- ☐ Help build into other couples what we have learned about God

- ☐ Memorize Scripture
- ☐ Prayer-walk together
- ☐ Attend church together
- ☐ Ask the Spirit to lead us as we recommit or ask for wisdom in this area: _____
- ☐ Fast for wisdom for a critical decision, for our marriage, or for our children

GETTING READY FOR DINNER
Preparation for Your Dinner and Dialogue Assignment

In preparation for your date this week, make a list of the people and situations you want to pray about with your lover. Bring this list to your date and spend time together asking God to work in a way that is beyond your ability.

People I would like us to pray for:	Situations I would like us to pray for:

LOVE LETTER

In your letter this week, thank your spouse for letting Jesus work in his or her life, and then finish these statements:

- I see God working in your life in the following ways…
- And it makes me feel…

Notes

1. Contributed by Rob Carpentier, *Reader's Digest*, February 1997, 15-16.

2. www.rd.com/clean-jokes-and-laughs/rear-love-to-rear-window-joke/article79368.html.

3. Karen Peterson, "Friendship Makes Marriages a Success," *USA Today*, April 1, 1999, quoting John Gottman, a researcher from the University of Washington.

4. Adapted from www.rd.com/clean-jokes-and-laughs/problem-solver/article41401.html.

■■■

For more resources to enhance your relationships
and build marriages or to connect with Bill and Pam Farrel
for a speaking engagement, contact

Farrel Communications
Masterful Living Ministries
3755 Avocado Boulevard, #414
La Mesa, CA 91941

800-810-4449

info@farrelcommunications.com

www.farrelcommunications.com

For help with marriage issues in midlife, visit
www.seasonedsisters.com

■■■